Growing Leaders

20 Articles to Challenge, Inspire, and Amplify Your Leadership

David Spungin

The **Leader Growth Group**

P.O. Box 2371 Evergreen, CO 80439

www.leadergrowthgroup.com

ISBN-13: 978-1974432233

ISBN-10: 1974432238

*This book is dedicated to
Carol Jarboe and Mark Spungin.*

Contents

Introduction

David Spungin

Hello and welcome! I'd like to start by acknowledging the remarkable period we are living in and how much opportunity our modern world offers us. This book is a testament to that opportunity. Just a decade ago, I may not have ever written it. With so many barriers to traditional authorship, getting my ideas out into the world seemed like wishful thinking. However, the rise of social media has since provided me with powerful platforms and disruptive technologies. With novel and innovative ways to reach new audiences, it is easy to connect with others who share similar passions and ideals. Fortunately, I realized the potential early on and jumped at the chance to share core insights from my twenty plus years of coaching and training leaders.

As my social media presence has grown, I've enjoyed interacting with many wonderful people from around the world. Some who graciously shared their feedback, both positive and constructive. Not surprisingly, several articles worked better for people than others. This book captures the best of the best...my top 20 articles thus far, representing some 110,000 views through LinkedIn alone at the time of this book's printing. Several articles have been republished in professional forums or translated into various languages to increase their reach. For many blogging giants in my field, this sort of attention is simply "par for the course." Yet, for me, I am deeply humbled by my reader's attentiveness. You have inspired me to think deeper and reach more people. This book is both an expression of my gratitude for your devotion, and represents my commitment to writing more significant works in the future.

How to Use This Book

While there may be no "one right way" to use this book, I'll offer a few thoughts based on how it's organized. Unlike a conventional book with a beginning, middle, and an end, the books chapters are not connected. Instead, it has six parts, each with three to four articles sharing common themes. You can start wherever you'd like. Perhaps there is a section that is of interest to you, or a chapter title that catches your eye. Feel free to jump around. Also, the chapters are not long. They are deliberately concise to aid the time-starved individual. My intent is for a leader to fit some professional development in while they have a few minutes on their commute, or perhaps as a productive way to start their day before jumping straight into their email.

Assess, Reflect, and Grow!

To add value to the articles, I've included a page at the end of each chapter called "Asses, Reflect, and Grow!" (which acts like a supplemental workbook). The format is derived from The Leader Growth Group's (LGG) Leader Development Process of 1) exposing leaders to new information, 2) providing space for reflection, and 3) encouraging leaders to act and learn from new experiences. To get the most out of the book, I encourage readers to leverage these pages.

One Simple Thing (OST)

You will notice that the final step of every "Assess, Reflect, and Grow!" page asks you to commit to one simple thing (OST). This step is critical, as it is only through action that we can enable embodied learning. So, what does "one simple thing" really mean? Think of it as a practice; something you can make tangible and measure. Something that is not so difficult that you won't really do it. Yet, not so easy that it doesn't push you outside your comfort zone. Every article has multiple ideas in it. Not everything will resonate with you, nor can you do everything that is offered. Pick something small and commit until you build a new habit. For example: If I just finished the article "Four Beliefs That Limit Your Leadership Potential," I might use the following as my OST...

For the next 14 days, I will identify areas in my work where I acknowledge I am not an expert. As a daily practice, I will reach out to my team members and try to ask two questions/day about these areas to hone my sense of curiosity and overcome my limiting belief that I am supposed to have all the answers.

It is through actionable and practical commitments like this that leaders get better and grow themselves. I know it's difficult, and you've likely got a million other things on your mind. Yet, if you are serious about your development, commit to these practices. Remember…No one can make you a better leader but you!

Finally, while every leader must accept responsibility for their own development, know that you are not alone on this journey and finding the right support is important. To learn more about how The Leader Growth Group can support you or your organization's professional development, contact me directly at dspungin@leadergrowthgroup.com.

Be Well and Lead Well,

The Leader Growth Group

David Spungin

David Spungin
Founder & Principal Consultant
The Leader Growth Group, LLC

Think Like **a Leader**

4 Beliefs That Limit Your Leadership Potential

*A **follower**, a **manager**, and a **leader** walk into a bar. They are all thirsty for a beer but the place is very crowded and it may take a while before they are served. Sure enough, many minutes pass and no one helps them. Feeling annoyed but unsure of what he can do, the follower continues to sit patiently for the waiter to arrive. Unhappy with waiting for the inefficient waiter to come by his table, the manager secures a menu from the hostess, analyzes the beer options, assesses the cost of an import vs. domestic beer, and finally signals his urgent readiness to order to the waiter across the room. Recognizing that there are three very thirsty people in her presence, the leader walks across the room to the bartender,* *communicates her need while extending a healthy tip, and returns to the table with three cold mugs and a frothy pitcher of delicious beer. Her absolutely delighted compatriots rejoice!*

Stereotypes aside, why would each individual take a very different course of action when they all wanted the same result? The answer lies in what possibilities we allow ourselves, and our realm of possibilities are a direct function of our belief systems. More succinctly put — **our values, beliefs, and personal stories drive our behavior**. The follower's personal story was one of limited possibilities. There were social norms that he was supposed to follow, and wanting to be a good follower, he did what he thought he was supposed to do. The manager's personal story is one of control. Valuing efficiency and optimization, he took action that would expedite the ordering process. The leader's personal story is one of service. Ignoring social norms and irrational restraints, the leader assessed the needs of the group, adapted to the environment, and made things happen through purposeful action. Why was the leader most effective? Because she was not confined by a story that limited her potential.

In my executive coaching work, I have come across several common beliefs that consistently show up and can limit a leader's potential. Note that these stories do not discriminate, and even the most successful leaders can sometimes fall victim to them periodically. My hope is that by sharing these with you, it may bring awareness to your own personal stories and how they impact your leadership potential. As you read these first four, check-in with yourself....what is it that you believe?

1. Leaders are supposed to have the answers

– Are we not? We get promoted to positions of authority primarily based on our experience and competence.

11

Followers value our ability to clearly articulate vision and direction. Thus, we are supposed to be the smartest person in the room. If you don't know, then you can't possibly be leading effectively. False! Not knowing is a prerequisite for curiosity, which enables both a sense of humility and our ability to innovate. Leaders who value curiosity over knowledge tend to facilitate the exchange of diverse perspectives and foster healthy debate within teams. Yet, leaders who can thrive in such ambiguity are a rare breed. For more on how you can overcome this common belief and instead turn uncertainty into opportunity, I recommend Steven D'Souza and Diana Renner's book, "Not Knowing."

2. Good leaders never show signs of

weakness – Of course they don't! As soon as you show weakness, the wolves will attack your soft underbelly. Great leaders project strength and have the will to overcome adversity. Well, this is only part of the story! Great leaders also know  how to demonstrate vulnerability to increase their approachability and authenticity with followers. In doing so, they connect with followers in a truly meaningful way and inspire far more engagement than the stoic warrior-leader ever could. Once more, leaders must know how to ask for help. No leader can succeed alone, and if you believe that asking for help is a sign of weakness, you have already significantly limited your potential.

3. My team can't operate without me – This one is

certainly the truth, right? The place falls apart when you go on vacation. Plus, we all know that things just won't get done right unless you are personally involved. Untrue! If anything, this is the manager's story not a leader's story. Leaders seek to relinquish control and recognize that the true mark of leadership is when they can walk away from a situation and trust that things will be executed in their absence. Why? Because leaders create more leaders. In the U.S. military, leaders are required to train multiple people to do their job should they be lost in battle. It is a culture that inspires constant coaching and mentoring. Your leadership ability then becomes more about the quality of your team than your personal skill. I wish I saw more of this in our modern corporate environments. Instead, I often come across leaders who believe that training the team too well makes them expendable. Do you need to be the hero? Or do you relish in creating heroes? Leaders value the latter.

Great Leaders Create More Leaders

www.leadergrowthgroup.com

4. It's my job as a leader to enforce the rules – This is a no brainer. Rules exist for a reason and leaders have a responsibility to ensure that team members work within the social contracts we agree upon. If they don't, the result is chaos and disorder. No organization can survive in such conditions. Not exactly! A leader must manage two operating systems: one that limits risk and one that encourages experimentation and change. Leaders fully own their responsibility to provide stability and act ethically. Yet, they also push boundaries and realize that sometimes rules exist to stifle innovation, preserve the status quo, and bring outliers right back to average. The mindset of a leader should always be one that abhors mediocrity. What's more important to you, meeting other's expectations or redefining the expectations altogether?

If any of these stories resonate with you personally, it may be time to release a belief or work towards changing a value that is no longer serving you as a leader. In part two of this article, I'll examine four more beliefs that can limit your potential as a leader, including the most pervasive belief that holds leaders back.

Assess, Reflect, and Grow!

1. Self-Assess

⇒ If someone asks you a question and you don't have the answer...what's your default?

1------------2-------------3-------------4-------------5-------------6-------------7
I get nervous and try to appear smart   I admit my ignorance and get curious

⇒ How often do you concede your known weaknesses to others?

1------------2-------------3-------------4-------------5-------------6-------------7
Never! Never! Never!   I'm an open book! Transparency builds trust

⇒ If you left for 2 weeks' vacation today, how well would your team continue to operate?

1------------2-------------3-------------4-------------5-------------6-------------7
Not well at all   Very Well, people are trained and empowered

⇒ What is your natural tendency as a leader?

1------------2-------------3-------------4-------------5-------------6-------------7
I encourage limited risk-taking   I encourage experimentation and initiative

2. Reflect

⇒ Which of these limiting beliefs show up for you most often?

_____

_____

_____

_____

_____

_____

⇒ Every limiting belief serves us in some way...How is this belief serving you?

_____

_____

_____

_____

_____

_____

3. Commit to New Growth

⇒ What is one simple thing (OST) you can practice to think more like a leader?

_____

_____

_____

_____

_____

_____

4 (More) Beliefs That Limit Your Leadership Potential

In part one of this article, we explored **how our values, beliefs, and personal stories drive our behavior** through the crowded bar story. After waiting a long time for service, the leader acted and secured a pitcher of beer for her thirsty team. Let's pick it up from there…

Finally enjoying their frothy cold beverages together, the **follower, manager**, *and* **leader** *begin to talk about their day. The follower starts the conversation by explaining his routine challenges to the group. Apparently, the sales team keeps over-promising on what his manufacturing team can deliver and the timid follower feels he can't speak up about it. The intense workload and impossible demands are taking their toll on him and his peers. He then describes his boss as a "slave* *driver" with no backbone to stand up to those "prima donna sales snobs!"*

Unfortunately, and unbeknownst to the follower, the gentleman to his left happens to be the head manager of sales and he is quickly becoming very defensive about the follower's tirade. The now irate manager begins to loudly express his strong denouncement of everything the follower has just shared. He then explains his intricate system for accurate sales forecasting, his impeccable record of always making his numbers, and how it's just too bad if the "whiny" manufacturing folks can't keep up!

At this point, the leader intervenes. First, she explains to the manager that she hears what he is saying and offers that the sales team is under a lot of pressure to deliver on the quarterly expectations. She then coaches the now very embarrassed follower into not backing down from this challenge by the manager. She expresses her interest in learning more about the follower's challenges and begins to facilitate the much-needed discussion. After a few uncomfortable minutes, the group begins to engage with each other and truly hear one another's needs and concerns. By the end of the night, they are toasting each other and commit to making several improvements together. The leader then picks up the tab and Ubers a cab for their ride home!

This brings us to the next four beliefs that can limit your potential as a leader. As you read through them, I offer that you 1) try to identify how these stories might be either limiting or working towards the leadership potential of our fictional characters in the bar scenario and 2) check in with your own beliefs and how they are shaping the possibilities available to you. **Again...what is it that you personally believe?**

1. I must be liked to be a good leader

- This makes perfect sense. Surly, no one wants to work with someone that they don't like. Besides, leadership is about

influence and how could I begin to influence people if they don't like me? If I work to be liked first, then people will go out of their way to help me and make me successful in my leadership responsibilities. *Not necessarily.* While being liked as a leader certainly helps, it should never be a primary motivator for your behavior. Leaders often must make tough decisions and sometimes those decisions will make them unpopular. Whether it be delivering news about much needed sacrifices ahead or having difficult accountability conversations, leaders must be comfortable with communicating the hard truth versus what will make people happy. **Instead of working to be liked, work to be respected.** Not in the sense that followers respect your authority, but rather respected for your competence, compassion, character, commitment, and consistency. The "liking" part will then take care of itself.

2. A leader ensures a harmonious team – Huh?

How could this not be true? We all know that harmony is a good thing. I mean, what kind of leader lets team members get into conflict with one another, which always has such a chilling  effect on the rest of the group? A leader's job is to ensure that various personalities on the team find a way to get along. *Not really!* It's very easy to fall into this trap as it is socially engrained in us from an early age. Groups naturally strive for harmony and the moment that conflict emerges, we just want it to go away. If a leader provides us with protection and re-establishes order in these moments, they are exercising authority not leadership![1] **Good leaders instead recognize that conflict is a necessary part of getting the group's needs met.** More importantly, leaders understand the ramifications of repressing conflict and promoting a false harmony — resentment and crippling dysfunction. Leaders instead create a trustful space for diverse perspectives to speak their truth and enable healthy debate to occur.

3. Leaders don't fail – Of course they don't fail! Failures fall by the wayside and it's those that succeed that are promoted to positions of greater responsibility and opportunity. Leadership and failure go together like oil and water. There is simply no mixing the two or you will quickly be labeled a poor leader. *Wrong!* Leaders are never one to play it safe. "Comfortable" is a dirty word to them and, thus, they take risks and push our boundaries to achieve what is possible. Yet, leaders, like everyone else, rarely get everything right the first time. They make mistakes, and it's how they handle  their mistakes that separate them from non-leaders. **Leaders never let their mistakes define them.** They don't avoid their failures, they own them and value them. Failures instead become powerful ways to expedite learning, strengthen resilience, and inspire an even greater will to succeed.

4. I'm not good enough to lead – Seriously, what were they thinking putting me in charge? I have been faking it the whole way. Sure, I had some successes, but anyone could have produced the same results. It's only a matter of time before they figure me out. *Absolutely, Positively, NO!* This may seem to be ridiculously obvious as a limiting belief; however, it is by far the #1 most pervasive belief holding many leaders back. Even many "successful" leaders share this story and, ironically, it can be the primary driver of their success. When this belief serves them, they work extra hard to overcome their insecurity and embrace continuous learning. Unfortunately, this story also can cause a leader to overcompensate for their ego, feeding almost every other belief discussed in this post! If this is resonating with you, know this; you are not alone and you don't need anything else. **You already have everything it takes to be an extraordinary leader.** The real challenge is will your willingness to internally validate yourself enough to be the leader that you are destined to become. When you flip the switch inside and see yourself as that leader – you are.

Leaders are those who can look beyond their own self-imposed limits.

www.leadergrowthgroup.com

Remember that our beliefs, values, and personal stories are not fixed. We can change them at any time. It's not a simple undertaking, yet it's certainly a worthwhile endeavor if they are limiting our leadership capacity. The world needs your leadership. **Choose to reach your full potential**.

Assess, Reflect, and Grow!

1. Self-Assess

⇒ How comfortable are you with making decisions that may make you unpopular?

1------------2-------------3-------------4-------------5-------------6-------------7
I hate it! Being liked is important to me   No problem, it comes with the territory

⇒ How comfortable are you with allowing conflict to occur within your team?

1------------2-------------3-------------4-------------5-------------6-------------7
I avoid conflict like the plague   Healthy debate only makes us better

⇒ How often do you stretch yourself to the point of failure?

1------------2-------------3-------------4-------------5-------------6-------------7
Failure...what's that?   I thrive in pushing my limits

⇒ How confident are you in your leadership abilities?

1------------2-------------3-------------4-------------5-------------6-------------7
Ugh! I'm quite bad at leading   I strongly believe in my ability to lead

2. Reflect

⇒ Which of these limiting beliefs show up for you most often?

_____

_____

_____

_____

_____

_____

⇒ Every limiting belief serves us in some way...How is this belief serving you?

_____

_____

_____

_____

_____

_____

3. Commit to New Growth

⇒ What is one simple thing (OST) you will practice to think more like a leader?

_____

_____

_____

_____

_____

_____

_____

4 Beliefs That Increase Your Leadership Potential

A follower, a manager, and a leader set out on a road trip together. After packing the car, they briefly discussed who should drive. Not wanting to be responsible for potentially getting them lost, the follower opts out and takes a spot in the back seat. Then, sensing the manager's need to be in control, the leader hands over the keys and instead reviews the map from the shotgun position. It wasn't very long into their adventure that everyone realized how they all were in the perfect place to best contribute. The leader was doing a fantastic job of monitoring congestion alerts, augmenting the route, and then providing clear directions to the manager. In turn, the manager, who was a superb driver, safely obeyed the traffic laws while skillfully weaving through the crowded highway. Finally, capitalizing on his natural gift for DJing, the follower played a great medley of tunes from his iPhone's extensive music collection that kept the group upbeat throughout. In fact, things were going so well that no one noticed that they were almost out of gas!

As their car slowly sputtered to the side of the road, the manager was livid as he had specifically asked the follower to fill the car with gas before they left and, the closest gas station was many miles away. The mood in the car now quickly turned sour as the manager angrily sought to hold the follower accountable for his mistake. The follower knew he had really screwed up. Sulking in his seat, he felt horrible. Evaluating what would best serve the group in this moment, the leader began to speak.

"Gentlemen, this is my fault. Prior to the trip, I asked the follower to help me load the car. He likely didn't have time to get gas because he was doing me a favor. What I thought would take only a few minutes ended up taking over an hour." The follower immediately felt better, not necessarily because he was no longer on the hook, but because he felt connected to the leader who was both sticking up for him and exercising personal accountability. Even the manager, while still not particularly happy about the situation, felt his emotions subside and was now more concerned with solving the problem.

Everyone then quickly got back to what they did best. The follower walked up and down the roadside to try and flag down someone who might help, the manager inventoried their resources available in case they were stranded for an extended period, and the leader got on the phone with AAA to try and secure towing support. Each bringing his diverse talents to the situation, it wasn't long before the group was back on the road and headed in the right direction again!

In my recent articles on eight beliefs that limit your leadership potential, we explored how our values, beliefs, and personal stories shape what possibilities are available to us and, thus, are responsible for driving our behavior. This then raises an important question. If there are certain beliefs that hold us back as leaders, are there certain beliefs that might enable us to better fulfill our leadership potential?

After 20+ years of studying leadership and observing some truly amazing leaders in action, I think there are certain beliefs that set the best leaders apart from the rest of their peers. These leaders understand that there are ways of looking at the world that will open possibilities, ensure priorities are maintained, and invite greatness. As you read through these first four beliefs, evaluate how they might have showed up in the story metaphorically and, if they are congruent with your own system of beliefs. If you assess these beliefs as your own, to what extent are they fully embodied? Check in with your daily actions as a leader...would others agree that your behavior is congruent with the following:

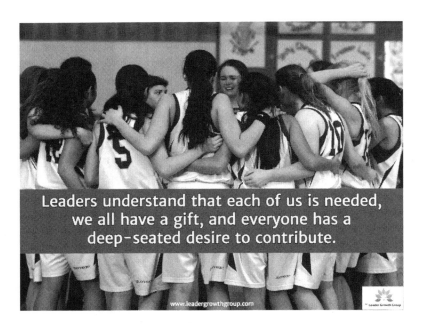

Leaders understand that each of us is needed, we all have a gift, and everyone has a deep-seated desire to contribute.

www.leadergrowthgroup.com

1. Everyone comes to this world with unique gifts to offer

– If you're a results-focused leader like I am, this may seem a little soft and sentimental. Yet, the reality is that each of us is needed, has value, and has a deep-seated desire to contribute. When we hold this belief, we no longer use people like human "resources" to be managed as we delegate work tasks. Instead, we seek to understand each person's gifts and how they can best be leveraged. A leader who truly embodies this belief at a core level will also look beyond an individual's surface level attributes. They become curious as to what gifts remain untapped, and wonder how this individual might contribute in ways that they haven't considered yet. The best leaders help us to see potential in ourselves that we never knew existed.

2. There is strength in diversity – People often fear what they do not understand. Thus, when it comes to hiring people in organizations and building work groups, people often surround themselves with those who are much like themselves. Doing so makes us feel more in control — enabling a sense of comfort and a greater semblance of predictability. Yet, the best leaders lean into the discomfort of surrounding themselves with a diverse

 team. They know that homogeneity leads to groupthink and, hence, they value the varied perspectives that diversity offers. They also value independent thinking and, thus, create cultures where dissent is both encouraged and appreciated. Great leaders know they will rise or fall depending on the quality of the team they lead. The saying often goes that A's hire A's while B's hire C's. Perhaps more appropriately, A's hire diverse A's while B's hire similar C's.

3. Nobody shows up to work to suck – When individuals are not meeting organizational standards, the first thing many managers are likely to do is judge them as non-performers and document their failures. Essentially, they are protecting themselves and externalizing blame for their non-performance. In fact, many managerial experts will tell you that the faster you rid yourself of non-performers, the more effective the organization will be.

While there may be some truth to this, I believe the best leaders see things differently. First, they get curious as to what their part is in the non-performance behavior and recognize that, as an accountable leader, they likely had something to do with it. Leaders don't ask "why is this person failing?" but rather "where have I failed this person?" Their curiosity emerges from the belief that nobody shows up to  work with intentions of sucking at their job. Something else is likely going on. Perhaps they are going through a difficult personal challenge at home, or maybe they are simply in the wrong position for their natural skill-sets. Whatever the situation, non-performers are almost always doing the very best they can, given their circumstances. A true leader will then find a way to make them successful again. I have seen it time and time again…the best leaders never leave anyone behind.

4. A leader's primary responsibility is to serve followers – While the responsibilities of holding authority are

 stressful and can take their toll on a manager, an elevated position within an organizational hierarchy is certainly not without its perks. There is the increased status, access to information, and the powerful feeling of being more in control of one's destiny. Sometimes, it's easy to forget that when riding the lofty winds of authority, it's the fans of loyal followers who are keeping you in flight! That's why this belief is supremely important in reaching your full potential. Leaders know that if they are to be successful, their followers must be successful first. Thus, the best leaders rarely think in terms of their own personal needs or agenda, but rather work tirelessly to uncover and meet the needs of their followers. The irony being that when you serve your followers well, they will bend over backwards to make you successful! Not because you are their manager with great authority, but because they respect your outstanding leadership in helping them to become their best.

Hopefully, these first four beliefs personally resonate with you and your leadership experiences. If so, you are likely already fulfilling much of your leadership potential. If not, remember that our beliefs, values, and personal stories are not fixed; we can change them. While not a simple undertaking, it's always a worthwhile endeavor to strive for greater leadership capacity. The world needs your leadership. Choose to reach your full potential.

Assess, Reflect, and Grow!

1. Self-Assess

⇒ How well do you know each of your team member's unique strengths and gifts?

1------------2-------------3-------------4-------------5-------------6-------------7
Not well, I barely know them   Very well, I take pride in knowing my people

⇒ How comfortable are you in working with someone who is very different than you?

1------------2-------------3-------------4-------------5-------------6-------------7
I'd rather not   I seek out diverse work partners

⇒ How quickly can you judge someone as a "non-performer?"

1------------2-------------3-------------4-------------5-------------6-------------7
Very quick to judge   Only after consistent patterns emerge

⇒ Do you instinctively put the needs of your followers before your own needs?

1------------2-------------3-------------4-------------5-------------6-------------7
Honestly, almost never do I serve others   Service to others defines my style

2. Reflect

⇒ Which of these beliefs do you already embody as a leader?

_____

_____

_____

_____

_____

_____

⇒ Which could you stand to "work on?"

_____

_____

_____

_____

_____

3. Commit to New Growth

⇒ What is one simple thing (OST) you will do to authentically demonstrate greater commitment to any of these beliefs?

_____

_____

_____

_____

_____

_____

4 (More) Beliefs That Increase Your Leadership Potential

In part one of this post, we explored how **our values, beliefs, and personal stories drive our behavior** through the road trip story. After running out of gas, each team member played a pivotal role in getting them back on the road. The story demonstrated how **certain beliefs open possibilities, ensure priorities are maintained, and invite greatness**.

The next four beliefs presented should further enhance your leadership potential. As you read through them, I offer that you check in with yourself and ask if they are congruent with your own system of beliefs. If you assess these beliefs as your own, to what extent are you living them in your day-to-day actions?

1. With issues of integrity, there is a clear right and wrong path – A leader's reputation is intimately linked with his or her decision-making ability. Yet, in our often fast-paced and volatile world, making good decisions has become more complex. As a result, today's leaders are becoming more comfortable with making decisions in "gray areas," where there is no clear right answer. However, when it comes to issues of integrity, there are no "gray areas," there is simply right and wrong. The basics of integrity may seem overly fundamental…of

 course leaders shouldn't lie, cheat, or steal! Yet, if you inventory the greatest leadership failures in recent memory, they almost always are a failure of character. In the U.S. alone, we can look at Bernie Madoff, Bill Clinton, Mark Hurd, or Joe Paterno

as prime examples. All were clearly competent in their leadership positions and very successful before they started to make small choices that ultimately led them down a dangerous path of self-delusion. As William James once said, **"It's the small choices that bear us irresistibly towards our destiny."** Leaders know their values, exercise self-control, and choose the harder right—every time, all the time.

2. A leader's primary role is to manage culture –
When you think of a great leader, what comes to mind? For many, this question conjures up images of the visionary who sees what we cannot, and then sets the strategy to get there. For others, they respect the tactical genius who gets things done where others cannot, the one who enables flawless execution and delivers results. Yet, **the best leaders believe their most important role is not to set the strategy or even sustain execution, but to manage the organization's culture.** Why? Strategy can shift with the wind. Execution, while undoubtedly important, is likely already the primary focus of the entire

management team. Yet, who is looking after the culture? Whose job is it to communicate the values? Who will teach us the rituals, share stories and legends, hold ceremonies, and shape our daily operating assumptions? All of which will determine how well we execute on our strategy! Who will answer this call? Leaders will.

3. Sometimes, great leadership is being a good follower – Those who are in positions of organizational authority are also the ones we expect to most often exercise leadership. Thus, one of the most difficult things for a manager to do is to simply get out of the way. Just because one may have power, title, or positional authority does not mean they are the most qualified to lead every time. Perhaps there are team members with expert knowledge or experiences that make them better suited to determine a path or outcome. Or maybe, there are team members that need to grow, and the manager's leadership is stifling that growth. For example, when I'm training a large group of equally amazing leaders in a workshop and they embark on a team challenge together, not everyone can be a leader. In these scenarios, great leadership is often recognizing when one is hindering the process rather than adding value to it. I find it inspiring to watch an often dominant and influential leader recognize this truth, and then step aside to make space for others. For an experienced manager, it may not be easy to let others take the lead. Yet, ironically, it can also be masterful leadership.

Great management is about control. Great leadership is about inspiration. Inspire your people and then get out of their way!

www.leadergrowthgroup.com

4. 80% of success is simply showing up – You've probably heard it before as this is a staple comment of most sales training programs. Yet, when it comes to leadership, your presence cannot be underestimated. **Like the back of a raffle ticket, you must be present to win!** Your physical presence as a leader is a service to those you lead as it enables accessibility and facilitates critical communication. More importantly, **how you spend your time is the single greatest indicator of what is important to you**. If you are constantly buried in the office because those emails must be answered, you are definitely telling your followers what you most care about. You are communicating, "my needs come first." Yet, every time you make a consistent effort to check in with your people, ask what their challenges are, what resources they need, and how you may be of service, you are demonstrating a commitment to putting your follower's needs first. People understand

that managers get busy, and that's exactly why making a deliberate effort to create a more human connection through your presence will inspire greater loyalty and motivation.

Hopefully, these beliefs personally resonate with you and your leadership experiences. If so, you are likely already fulfilling much of your leadership potential. If not, remember that our beliefs, values, and personal stories are not fixed. We can change them at any time. While not a simple undertaking, it is always a worthwhile endeavor to strive for greater leadership capacity. The world needs your leadership. **Choose to reach your full potential.**

Assess, Reflect, and Grow!

1. Self-Assess

⇒ Do you consider yourself a leader of uncompromising integrity?

1------------2-------------3-------------4-------------5-------------6-------------7
It's not my strong suit   Without a doubt

⇒ How much attention do you regularly give to maintaining your organization's culture?

1------------2-------------3-------------4-------------5-------------6-------------7
I rarely think about culture   My primary focus is culture

⇒ How comfortable are you with giving away your power to other team members?

1------------2-------------3-------------4-------------5-------------6-------------7
Why would I do that?   Very comfortable when necessary

⇒ How accessible are you as a leader?

1------------2-------------3-------------4-------------5-------------6-------------7
I am private and sometimes aloof   I am present for others, physically and mentally

2. Reflect

⇒ Which of these beliefs do you already embody as a leader?

_____

_____

_____

_____

_____

_____

⇒ Which could you stand to improve on?

_____

_____

_____

_____

_____

3. Commit to New Growth

⇒ What is one simple thing (OST) you can do to authentically demonstrate greater commitment to any of these beliefs?

_____

_____

_____

_____

_____

_____

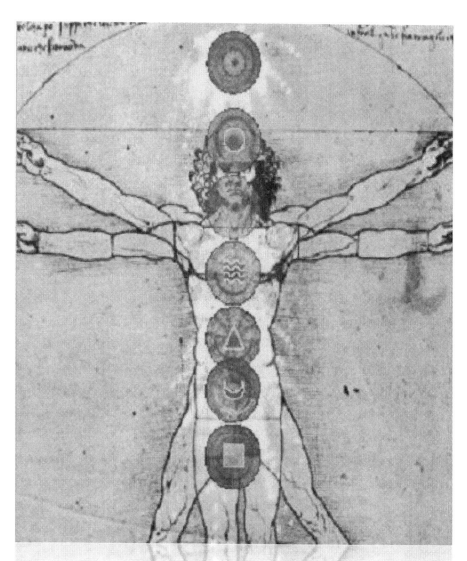

Body, Language,
and Emotions

Oh No! I Just "Got Hooked"... Now What?

Have you ever been "hooked" by another individual? Most of us have, and it usually happens with those that we deem to be "difficult" personalities. Sometimes, these people are very different from us, other times the issue is that they are **too much like us**. Usually, it's something they do or say that triggers the "hooking" inside us. Perhaps it was that insensitive comment in front of the team that poked you the wrong way. Or maybe it was the passive aggressive e-mail that really got under your skin. Whatever the reason or context, getting "hooked" is that moment when you realize **you are no longer fully in control**.

Something else is influencing your behavior. Try as you might to think rationally and behave with calmness, the body begins to interrupt. You may notice your heart rate increasing, sweaty palms or a dry mouth, or even your muscles tightening. What you are experiencing is the body's fight-or-flight stress response. While this deeply ingrained survival mechanism worked well with circumventing the dangers we faced 200,000 years ago, it's not exactly the ideal state to be in when trying to work through modern relationship challenges. Just when you need to be at your best and deal with the complexity of interpersonal dynamics, your body is narrowing its focus and operating with its prehistoric reptilian brain. Great, so now that we are behaving like a threatened lizard... what next?

At a subconscious level, **"getting hooked" nearly always is connected to feelings or emotions related to power, authority, inclusion, and/or trust.** Yet, one will never be able to recognize what is really going on if they are psychologically and physiologically limited through being "hooked." Thus, before assessing the situation and taking any action, the goal is to first **return to a state of centered presence**. Quickly accessing a centered presence is a particularly important skillset for a leader to master. It's important to remember that a leader is "always on a stage" and even just one reactive and unprofessional outburst can adversely impact one's credibility. So how can a leader find their center under stress? Here are some thoughts:

1. Stop and notice - The most important thing you can do to get "unhooked" is to shine the light on what's happening to you. Your body wants to move towards or away from the perceived threat, so **interrupt the instinct by imposing stillness**. Then just notice all the symptoms of the stress response. How fast is your heart beating? Are you sweating anywhere? Are you clenching your jaw or narrowing your brow?

2. Get out of your head and into your body - Your

thoughts about this individual are sparking the emotional reaction. Thus, you need to get out of your head's incessant replaying of the past event and anticipation of what might be in the future. Noticing

and then purposefully pacing your breath is perhaps the best way to bring yourself back to the present and regain control. You'll want to inhale through your nose deep into the belly (versus chest), and then exhale through your mouth. Your mind will

likely try to highjack you throughout this process, so keep your **focus on nothing but your breath entering and exiting your body**. If you can do so, closing your eyes or retreating to a quiet place momentarily is helpful.

3. Ground yourself - The mind and body are intimately

connected. Thus, if your mind is currently driving your body's

reaction, then it makes sense that shifting the body might conversely change the mind. Hence, sit up straight with the small of your back against the seat. Plant your feet firmly into the ground. Place the palm of your hands on your thighs and keep

your chin level. **Root yourself into the world and find your calm confidence**.

4. Find your center - Now that you are ready to be the

leader that is needed in this moment, it's time to assess your options

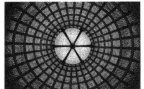

for action. Yet, mindset is an important part of this process. If you are not careful, your thoughts might quickly spin you up again into a state of being "hooked." Thus, first ask yourself what you are grateful for in this

world? This can be a powerful question to keep your head out of the clouds and emotions positive. Then remember that there are few things in this world that we can control. Often, the one and only thing that we have complete control over is our own behavior. It's important to note that whatever course of action you choose to take, it should be delivered from a service-based leadership mentality and executed with humility.

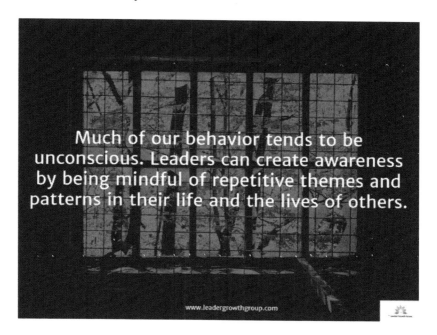

Much of our behavior tends to be unconscious. Leaders can create awareness by being mindful of repetitive themes and patterns in their life and the lives of others.

www.leadergrowthgroup.com

Finally, don't wait until the next time you get "hooked" to try this out. Returning to a centered presence is a highly complex and challenging skill for a leader to master. It takes a lot of practice in each of these skill subsets to pull it all together, particularly when under stress. Yet, with the alternative being subject to one's lizard brain, it might be a worthwhile investment!

Assess, Reflect, and Grow!

1. Self-Assess

⇒ How quickly do you become aware of when you get "hooked" by something?

1------------2-------------3-------------4-------------5-------------6---------7
Days Afterwards   Almost Instantly

⇒ How practiced are you at "centering yourself" in difficult moments?

1------------2-------------3-------------4-------------5-------------6-------------7
Never tried it   Expert proficiency

⇒ How much do you pay attention to your body language in each moment?

1------------2-------------3-------------4-------------5-------------6-------------7
Little to no awareness   I consciously shape myself to meet my intent

2. Reflect

⇒ Think of something that "hooked you" recently....what happened?

_____

_____

_____

_____

_____

⇒ What were the underlying causes of you getting "hooked?"

_____

_____

_____

_____

_____

_____

⇒ How did you react? If you could "re-do" your reaction, how would it sound?

_____

_____

_____

_____

_____

_____

3. Commit to New Growth

⇒ What is one simple thing (OST) you will do next week to help you to avoid being hooked in the future and maintain a centered presence?

_____

_____

_____

_____

_____

_____

The Tyranny of the "But"
The Genius of the "And"

Put yourself in the following scenario. You are in a strategy discussion with several colleagues and everyone has their own idea as to the most effective way forward for the team. Thus, everyone engages in a healthy debate as to what makes the most sense. You have the floor and begin to passionately convey your message. You lay out a sound, lucid, and emotionally convincing plan that is sure to captivate your fellow team members. Across the table is Pat, who has been anxiously waiting for you to finish. You have barely ended your thought when Pat says, "I hear what you are saying, **but**..." You could insert any number of ways to finish this sentence; however, this might prove difficult as you are probably not paying much attention to what Pat is saying at this point.

The word "but" is a word that every leader should try to avoid altogether. It is the fastest way to shut another person down and have them put up their defensive walls to your ideas. The word "but" signals to others that you are an either/or type thinker. **Either** we adopt your idea **or** we go with mine. When either/or thinkers  communicate, the word "but" often serves as a transition to convincing others as to why their idea will not work. The result is a loss of influence, something every leader wants to avoid.

So how can a leader express a difference of opinion or an alternate point of view? The answer is a simple shift in language that has a profound impact. **Leaders replace the word "but" with the words "yes, and" when communicating alternative points of view.** Some examples might include:

1. "**Yes**, I really like that idea for delivering a short-term boost to profits, **and** it is really important we think about the long-term impacts of such a decision. What might some of those be?"

2. "**Yes**, I agree that lowering our costs is very important in this market, **and** we might be more likely to suffer quality issues as a result... how could we avoid this?"

3. "**Yes**, I am seeing how this change strategy could work, **and** I am mindful that we have some traditional practices that work very well for us... what do we need to preserve?"

 By acknowledging the other person's thoughts first with the simple affirmation of "yes," and then adding to them through thought provoking questions, the leader will lessen the defensiveness of others and gain greater influence. In essence, the leader is **modeling the energy of openness that they need from others if their own ideas are to be truly heard**. Others will notice this shift in presence and language, and then return that energy to the leader.

The result is often a group that seeks to build off one another's ideas versus digging in and holding their personal position.

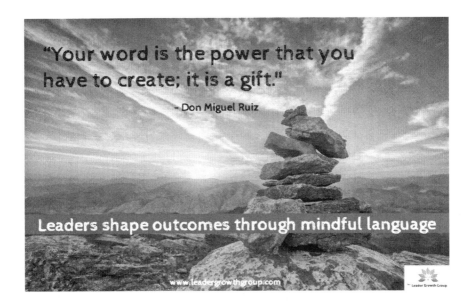

Thus, be mindful of when either/or thinking shows up for you as a leader and instead insert this easy, yet impactful, shift in language. You will be sure to increase your influence and persuasive abilities.

Assess, Reflect, and Grow!

1. Self-Assess

⟹ When a team member presents an idea, do you like to play devil's advocate?

1------------2-------------3-------------4-------------5-------------6-------------7
Yes! I'm quite good at it   I usually try to build off other's ideas instead

⟹ How often do you "need to be right" when debating ideas?

1------------2-------------3-------------4-------------5-------------6-------------7
I'll fight to the death!   I am very open to other's ideas

⟹ How often do you use the word "but" when making a counter-point?

1------------2-------------3-------------4-------------5-------------6-------------7
Way more than I probably should   I consciously avoid it

2. Reflect

⟹ Think of a recent debate you've had... What was the other person's point of view?

_____

_____

_____

_____

⇒ How could you have empathized with their point, <u>and</u> made your point, by using the language of "yes, I understand you feel…, and I….?"

_____

_____

_____

_____

_____

_____

_____

_____

_____

3. Commit to New Growth

⇒ Try this one simple thing (OST) as a practice. Count how many times you use the word "but" vs. the words "Yes, and" for 7 days. Track your results daily at the end of each day and then total the number for the week. How did you do? How can you keep this top of mind until "but" no longer becomes part of your vocabulary!

_____

_____

_____

_____

_____

_____

_____

_____

_____

_____

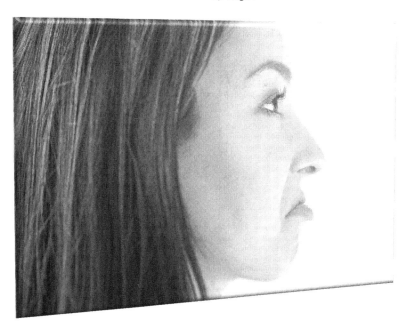

A Positive Outlook on Negativity

Look on the bright side of things! Who can argue with that philosophy? We all inherently understand the impact of both positive and negative emotions in the workplace. Optimistic "can do" personalities tend to bring us energy whereas negative moods and emotions can drain an organizational system. This phenomenon is especially relevant when discussing how a leader can impact a situation. Leaders often set the emotional tone within the workplace, either inspiring others to reach higher or sabotaging the team with emotions such as doubt, disappointment, and/or anger.

Yet, is it ever good for a leader to experience and express negative emotions? Perhaps. As a leader, we should strive to be highly cognizant of our negative emotions for several reasons. Yes, they can have a chilling effect on our team if left unchecked, but they can also bring us moments of insight if we have the self-awareness and courage to examine their underpinnings. A mindful leader recognizes their own mood or negative emotion in the moment and asks, "I wonder what this is all about?" As an executive coach, I have asked many leaders this very question when they experience negative emotions. Here are some of the most common responses and insights.

1. Doubt - This is an important emotion for a leader because it alerts us to risk of loss. **Without doubt, we would have difficulty in maintaining any focus as endless possibilities would constantly distract us**. A little doubt in our lives enables us to prioritize use of our energy and, more importantly, identify where we need to refocus our resources to ensure the team's success.

2. Disappointment – Often, we feel disappointment when a standard or expectation has been violated within the team. Sometimes, we may not even be conscious of these expectations until we feel the disappointment. **These feelings will often compel a leader to communicate expectations that might not otherwise have been voiced**. In this way, disappointment becomes the catalyst for difficult conversations to occur, which will ultimately improve performance.

3. Anger - What good could possibly come from anger? Lots. Anger tells us what we really care about, what we value, and what needs our immediate attention. **Leaders experiencing anger may also feel motivated to act when they might otherwise not**. When the leader can channel that energy away from a need to punish and more towards a need for resolution, it becomes a powerful force in driving results.

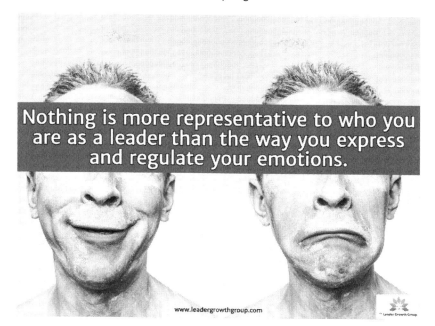

Nothing is more representative to who you are as a leader than the way you express and regulate your emotions.

www.leadergrowthgroup.com

Responsible use of negative emotions, like most things in life, is about balance. It is only through experiencing crippling doubt that we know what true confidence really means. In feeling utter disappointment, we recognize pure satisfaction. It is through fiery anger that we learn the importance of patience, peacefulness, and self-control. **A savvy and mindful leader does not strive for an absence of negative emotions; rather s/he pays attention to these powerful cues and makes them a positive source of insight.**

Assess, Reflect, and Grow!

1. Self-Assess

⟹ How often do you experience doubt in the workplace?

1------------2-------------3-------------4-------------5-------------6-------------7
Rarely   Everyday

⟹ How often do you experience disappointment in the workplace?

1------------2-------------3-------------4-------------5-------------6-------------7
Rarely   Everyday

⟹ How often do you experience anger in the workplace?

1------------2-------------3-------------4-------------5-------------6-------------7
Rarely   Everyday

2. Reflect

⟹ Which of these emotions do you express most often?

_____

_____

_____

_____

_____

_____

⇒ What's underneath this emotion? What is it telling you?

_____

_____

_____

_____

⇒ How did you express this emotion?

_____

_____

_____

_____

⇒ Did your expression serve you as a leader?

_____

_____

_____

_____

3. Commit to New Growth

⇒ What is one simple thing (OST) you will practice to better understand negative emotions in the workplace and how they can inform your leadership?

_____

_____

_____

_____

_____

Be a Mood Barometer

Photo Credit: James E. Petts

Have you ever walked into a meeting and felt as if the temperature dropped a few degrees? Not literally, yet it just felt colder, as if there was a drafty cloud of anxiety or standoffishness hanging in the air. How about the other way around? You jump on a team call and you sense an instantaneous feeling of warmth, informing you that this was a space of caring and possibilities. What you are sensing in these moments is "the mood in the room" and, as a leader, it is important to master the subtleties of this emotional intelligence skill-set.

Savvy leaders can quickly assess "the mood in the room" and adjust their communication to best influence others.

So how do we increase our ability to consciously assess the collective mood of a group? The good news is that your body is naturally equipped with all the tools necessary to do so. Your five senses are constantly taking in and assessing information. Is the room loud or quiet? Do you see people alone or in groups? Even try to notice what the colors and textures of people's clothing are telling you. Still, the greatest mood-sensing tool we have is our sixth sense; some refer to this as our gut intuition. To tap this resource, the leader must focus their attention away from what they are thinking, and more towards what they are feeling. In doing so, the leader becomes attuned to the energy in the room.

With greater energy awareness, a leader can then make the adjustments necessary to maximize their personal influence. For example, perhaps in sensing that the team's mood is one of high frustration and low energy at the end of the day, the leader chooses to abandon his initial intent of discussing the lagging sales numbers. Pressing forward with this agenda item at this moment would likely result in defensiveness and bickering over who's to blame for the poor results. The savvy leader recognizes both the importance of holding these crucial accountability conversations and the impact of mood when it comes to creating space for a healthy dialogue to occur. There is typically never a perfect time to hold these challenging conversations, and, yet, there are markedly better times than others.

So, what do you do if you simply can't wait for a group's mood to change? **The truly skilled leader will demonstrate their ability to shift their own personal mood and be the energy that is needed at that moment.** For instance, in meeting with a disgruntled client, the leader notices a heavy energy and feeling of distance between her team and the client's team. She may even feel awkward herself as she is holding on to several "hidden" issues she has with the client.

Here, the leader might adjust from jumping straight into technical problem solving and instead deliberately open themselves up while expressing these concerns. She would consciously shift her mood to one of authenticity, calmness, and warmth to be most effective.

She might then offer, "I wonder if it might be helpful if we spend a few minutes upfront to check in with one another. I feel as if we both may have some unspoken frustrations, and I would really appreciate hearing what's on your mind. Please know that we all deeply care about your team and this project's success...let's chat a bit before we jump into the project milestones." While the client's team may then vent their frustrations passionately, our leader models the energy needed to keep the relationship intact and the project moving forward.

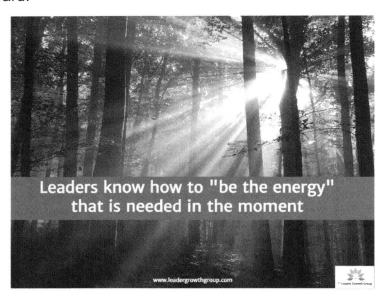

Leaders know how to "be the energy" that is needed in the moment

www.leadergrowthgroup.com

Mastering the art of being a mood barometer is a challenging skill for even the most seasoned leaders. Often, it takes years of life experience to calibrate your personal instrument. Yet, with enough deliberate practice, anyone can get better at this important skill that distinguishes great leaders from the rest of the pack.

Assess, Reflect, and Grow!

1. Self-Assess

⟹ How skilled are you at quickly assessing the "mood in a room?"

1------------2-------------3-------------4-------------5-------------6-------------7
I'm rather oblivious   I sense moods immediately

⟹ How skilled are you at changing your own energy to meet the needs of a group?

1------------2-------------3-------------4-------------5-------------6-------------7
I've never tried it   I can change my energy easily

2. Reflect

⟹ When was the last time you noticed a "group's mood"?

_____

_____

_____

_____

⟹ How did you adjust your communication to meet the needs of the group?

_____

_____

_____

_____

⇒ Can you recall a time when you were not tuned in to a group's mood? What happened?

_____

_____

_____

_____

_____

_____

_____

⇒ What do you personally pay attention to when assessing the "mood in a room?"

_____

_____

_____

_____

_____

_____

_____

3. Commit to New Growth

⇒ What is one simple thing (OST) you will do to help you in shifting your own energy to meet the collective mood of a group?

_____

_____

_____

_____

_____

_____

From **Battlefield**
to the **Boardroom**

5 Leadership Lessons I Learned at West Point

The United States Military Academy at West Point is one of the world's finest leadership laboratories. From the very first day (called R-Day for Reception day) that a new cadet enters the West Point system, they are immersed in a four-year-long formal leader development process that has been honed through 212 years of experimentation. Twenty-one years ago, I began my West Point journey and the subsequent four years taught me countless leadership lessons for which I am forever grateful. In this two part series, I have compiled some of the stickiest of these lessons that continue to guide me as a leader today.

1. Don't point the finger, point the thumb – At West Point, you are taught the first rule of leadership is everything is your fault! While this may sound just a bit harsh, it's not far from

the truth. As a leader, you are responsible for all your team does or fails to do. When mistakes happen, one's natural reaction is often to pass blame on to others or offer excuses. As a new cadet, you are allowed only four responses to questions, Yes, Sir; No, Sir; Sir, I do not understand; and No Excuse, Sir! This taught us to be accountable for our actions and question our own role in a team failure.

2. A leader is always on parade – Drill and ceremony is a central part of West Point's curriculum and watching the Corps of Cadets conduct a parade on the hallowed plain of West Point is a sight to behold. 4000 young men and women in their most formal uniforms all marching in complete synchronicity. As a cadet, all eyes are on you to do your part and do it well. It is the embodiment of situational awareness and

Photo by Mike Strasser

personal discipline. When in a leadership position — every day is parade day. You are constantly being watched and assessed by your followers. People are counting on you to do the right thing, when it should be done, and without being told to do it.

3. Embrace the suck – Cadet life can be tough and full of irony. The worse the weather, the more you are required to be out in it. No matter which way you have to

march, it always seems uphill. You have two choices. Either move towards the struggle and allow it to sharpen you, or let it consume you and break you down mentally. Leaders must do the same with their teams. Worthwhile goals always require an element of struggle and there will be moments when things downright suck for your team. Be a beacon of hope in times of adversity and always be compassionate with followers' challenges.

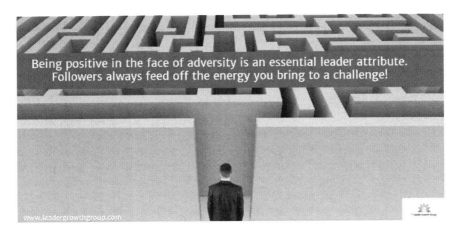

Being positive in the face of adversity is an essential leader attribute. Followers always feed off the energy you bring to a challenge!

www.leadergrowthgroup.com

4. No plan survives first contact – One essential skill every officer must learn is the art of planning and communicating orders. Cadets memorize specific frameworks like the 8 Steps to Troop Leading Procedures and the 5 Paragraph Operations Order to assist them in this process. Using these processes, an officer can spend days mapping out the best course of action, gathering intelligence, and synchronizing resources. Yet, real world experience soon teaches us that the  enemy always has a vote and plans often fall apart (and quickly). Likewise, strategy will always be an important part of today's business processes. Yet, the best companies today are adaptable and flexible with their environments. Leaders know when to abandon the plan and nimbly adjust to new circumstances.

5. People don't care how much you know until they know how much you care – West Point recruits some of the smartest kids in America. The average SAT score for the Class of 2018 was 1,270, and 82 of the 1,212 admitted were their high school's Valedictorian[2]. Yet, cadets quickly learn that people follow heart before head. Leaders must be servants to their followers and demonstrate that they are committed to putting the team before self. Competence and intelligence are important, but character defines you.

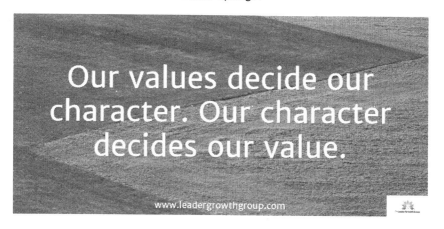

In essence, great leadership is about demonstrating personal accountability, acting with integrity, proving resilience, embracing adaptability, and embodying a mindset of selfless-service. The good news is that you don't have to go to West Point to learn these lessons. Anyone can adopt these behaviors and become a better leader. All it takes is choosing to lead differently and a commitment to practice consistently.

Assess, Reflect, and Grow!

1. Self-Assess

⇒ When mistakes happen on your team, what's your natural tendency?

1-----------2-------------3-------------4-------------5-------------6-------------7
Pass blame and offer excuses   Take full responsibility

⇒ How mindful are you to "be the example" of your own expectations for team members?

1-----------2-------------3-------------4-------------5-------------6-------------7
It's not a priority   Always!

⇒ How often do you challenge your team with big goals that create adversity?

1-----------2-------------3-------------4-------------5-------------6-------------7
We like to be comfortable   We "embrace the suck"

⇒ How difficult for you is it for you to change direction when executing a plan?

1-----------2-------------3-------------4-------------5-------------6-------------7
Like turning a battleship   Nimble as a cheetah

⇒ How often do you exhibit compassion in the workplace?

1-----------2-------------3-------------4-------------5-------------6-------------7
I don't do "kumbaya"   Every. Single. Day.

2. Reflect

⇒ Which of these leadership lessons are you already skilled at? Which could you work on?

_____

_____

_____

_____

_____

_____

_____

_____

_____

_____

3. Commit to New Growth

⇒ What is one simple thing (OST) you will do to practice one of these lessons at work?

_____

_____

_____

_____

_____

_____

_____

_____

_____

_____

5 (More) Leadership Lessons I Learned at West Point

The United States Military Academy at West Point has produced some of the United States' finest leaders. From President's Ulysses Grant and Dwight Eisenhower to General's Douglass MacArthur and George Patton, every graduate experiences a formal four-year Leader Development process that is designed to yield principled centered leaders of character. As a Leader Development professional and graduate myself, I often reflect on my West Point experience and the powerful leadership lessons that it taught me. In this two-part series, I compiled some of the stickiest lessons that continue to guide me today. Part one explored how great leadership is about demonstrating personal accountability, acting with integrity, proving resilience, embracing adaptability, and embodying a mindset of selfless-service. Here are five more timeless lessons to reflect on:

1. No combat ready unit ever passed inspection –

West Point cadets endure lots of inspections. From daily uniform checks to white glove room inspections called SAMI (Saturday Morning Inspection), by default, every cadet becomes a master shoe shiner and sink scrubber. If at any time you failed to meet Academy standards, you could get written up and ultimately end up walking hours on the area as punishment. No matter how "squared away" you were, most cadets end up walking at least a few hours over their four years as you are constantly juggling many priorities and eventually balls  are dropped. Thus, cadets get very good at prioritizing what is most important. With only so many hours in a day, sometimes, studying for the big exam or writing that important paper meant you would likely be written up for an untidy room or uniform. The same goes for leaders today. **It's important to get the big stuff right — always**. You might take a few bruises along the way, but in the long run, your ability to stay focused on what's most important will pay off.

2. Trust but Verify – In their second year at the Academy,

each cadet is assigned a first-year cadet (called a plebe) as a direct report. For many, this is his or her first opportunity to lead someone on a daily basis. You are responsible for your plebe's performance and quickly learn to conduct periodic inspections to ensure discipline  and proper accountability. While subordinates in today's organizations don't want leaders hovering over their shoulders and inspecting their every move, they do expect you to check in with them often and acknowledge their hard work. **Train your team, trust they will deliver, and then verify standards have been met**. The act of verification is important because it validates your leadership priorities and helps to clarify expectations for the team.

Photo by Tommy Gilligan/USMA PAO

3. There are no stupid questions when you are learning something new

– As a first-year cadet, success is often clouded with mystery. There is so much to learn and so little time to learn it all. Then, just when you think you have it all figured out, you are challenged with new tasks that make you feel like a novice again. To survive this intense period of learning, you must accept your vulnerabilities and lean into others for support (we used the saying "*Cooperate and Graduate*" as a reminder). Leaders today must do the same. No one expects you to have all the answers in this fast changing and complex world we live in. Instead, **leaders should practice an impassioned curiosity and have the courage to say "I don't know" when appropriate**. The irony being, in admitting our vulnerability, we often find the answers and/or develop the very competence we are seeking.

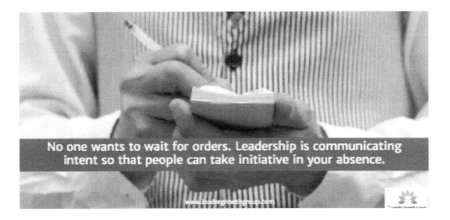

No one wants to wait for orders. Leadership is communicating intent so that people can take initiative in your absence.

www.leadergrowthgroup.com

4. Always understand your mission two levels up –

A key philosophy of U.S. Army operations is that in the absence of specific direction, any soldier should be able to take initiative and complete the mission. To support this concept, every officer learns to embrace their Commander's Intent, as well as their next level Commander's Intent. It might seem like overkill, but in the fog of war, intent is the glue that keeps a unit together. The corporate world is no different. For a leader to be successful, they need to make their supervisor and their organization successful. **Clearly understanding your bosses' definition of success, daily priorities, and leadership philosophy is a must.**

5. Mission first, people always – This popular Army slogan represents much of what a cadet does daily until it

philosophically permeates every bone in their body over time. From simply checking on your subordinates' feet while on a long road march, to never leaving a soldier behind on the battlefield, cadets practice balancing mission execution with taking care of their people's needs. Leaders in the corporate world should also embrace this philosophy. **Talent is the single greatest differentiator in the marketplace today and every organization's greatest asset is its people.** Successful business leaders understand how to manage the stresses of short-term stakeholder expectations while continuously being mindful of employee needs and concerns.

Thus, in addition to the behaviors noted in part one, great leadership is also about rigorously maintaining priorities, holding others accountable to standards, being a life-long learner, exercising initiative through intent, and taking care of your people at all times. It's worth repeating that you don't have to go to West Point to learn these lessons. Anyone can adopt these behaviors and become a better leader. Practice these behaviors consistently and watch your personal, team's, and organization's success exponentially increase.

Assess, Reflect, and Grow!

1. Self-Assess

⇒ How comfortable are you with "dropping some balls" to get the big stuff right?

1------------2-------------3-------------4-------------5-------------6-------------7
I'm a tactical perfectionist   I am strategic realist

⇒ How often do you follow up with subordinates and verify standards have been met?

1------------2-------------3-------------4-------------5-------------6-------------7
Rarely, I'm too busy   Always, it's a habit for me

⇒ How comfortable are you with asking questions in public when you don't understand?

1------------2-------------3-------------4-------------5-------------6-------------7
Very uncomfortable   It doesn't bother me at all

⇒ How clear is your bosses' boss definition of success, daily priorities, and philosophy?

1------------2-------------3-------------4-------------5-------------6-------------7
I have zero clarity   I thoroughly understand

⇒ What's more important to you...completing your mission or your taking care of people?

1------------2-------------3-------------4-------------5-------------6-------------7
Mission   People

2. Reflect

⇒ Which of these leadership lessons are you already skilled at? Which could you work on?

_____

_____

_____

_____

_____

_____

_____

_____

_____

_____

_____

3. Commit to New Growth

⇒ What is one simple thing (OST) you will do to practice one of these lessons at work?

_____

_____

_____

_____

_____

_____

_____

_____

_____

_____

_____

_____

Connect, Adapt, Collaborate: Applying Army Mission Execution Fundamentals to Business

Photo by Tech. Sgt. Russell E. Cooley IV.

The U.S. Army has a timeless and sticky saying used to drive home the fundamentals of mission execution. From the very first days of boot camp, a young Private will hear the Drill Sergeants yelling **"you must learn how to shoot, move, and communicate if you want to survive on the battlefield!"** They then go on to spend weeks mastering their personal weapon, learning how to low crawl and find cover, and practicing how to speak properly on the radio. Over time, one learns how important these skills really are. Yes, there are many more advanced competencies to learn over the course of your career, but if you can't do these three basics consistently well... it might all be for nothing.

These ideas are not limited to the military and there is much that corporate leaders can take away from this simple saying as well. Successfully executing any strategy, whether it is on the battlefield or in the boardroom, is often a function of doing the fundamentals consistently well. So how might the Army's fundamentals of shoot, move, and communicate apply to the modern business environment? There are many similarities, but I would translate the language to **connect, adapt, and collaborate**.

1. Connect - Just like the Private learning how to "put steel on target" at the weapons qualification range, business execution requires one to master their resources and connect them with distant objectives. Specifically, there are **three connections** to be made that foster better execution. First, master an awareness of your personal strengths and **connect**

these innate talents with the team's objectives. Ask yourself: *what are my exceptional gifts to the world and how can I provide the most value in day-to-day execution?* Next, smartly connect to the infinite resources outside of you. Who can do this challenging activity much better than you can? Savvy leaders realize their limitations and artfully **connect with others that complement those limitations**. Finally, fully **connect with your customer's needs and expectations**. Little is more frustrating than executing well on something that is no longer in the greatest service to your key stakeholders. Like the bullet seeking its target, the energy of connecting with your customer is one of laser-like focus. Don't wait for feedback; be proactive and purposeful in continuously reaching out to clarify how things are going.

2. Adapt - Successful execution is becoming less of a formulaic process, and maintaining flexibility and agility is increasingly important. We must practice our ability to move with our shifting environment and change plans as necessary. In the Army, we might rehearse a complex mission for weeks on end. Yet, we lived by the rules of "the enemy always has a

vote" and "no plan ever survives first contact (with that enemy)." A more relevant example might be at Google, where the culture promotes the concept of "design and iterate." Googlers see strategy and execution as being one - a continuously refined process of trial and error that speeds up results. We might intuitively understand these concepts; however, many find them difficult to implement. We frequently become wed to our brilliant plans or overly comfortable with stale execution processes. The key to overcoming these barriers is to **cultivate a "beginner's mind" and learn to approach potential change from a place of curiosity**. When we already "know" how to execute best, we resist things that do not reinforce these beliefs. Yet, **when we lose our rigidity and get curious about possibilities, change becomes a way to simply get better**.

3. Collaborate - Great execution today requires increased communication and collaboration. It seems simple enough, yet why can it be so hard to collaborate during execution? The answer lies in the two very different energies required to do these equally imperative skills. When we are personally executing, our heads are down, our eyes narrow, and we concentrate our energy so that we might overcome obstacles and complete our tasks. When we are collaborating, we pick our heads up, we  open our eyes wide, and seek to see the bigger picture around us. Executing and collaborating well is an ebb and flow of contraction and expansion. We collaborate to build intent, execute initial steps, communicate needs, execute some more, check in on collective progress, drive towards results... it's a rhythm we all know well. Yet, we all seem to do much better at the personal execution part than we do at the collaboration part. **Key to becoming a better collaborator is becoming aware of when you contract. When do you tend to put your head down and get overly focused on your piece of the execution pie?** For me, I contract when I have made a personal commitment and am up against a tight deadline.

In these moments, I can be a lousy communicator as I focus myself on fulfilling my promises and shut down to others in the process. Stress in general can make us all contract, so recognizing when we are stressed is a tell-tale sign that we need to communicate our needs and collaborate more with others.

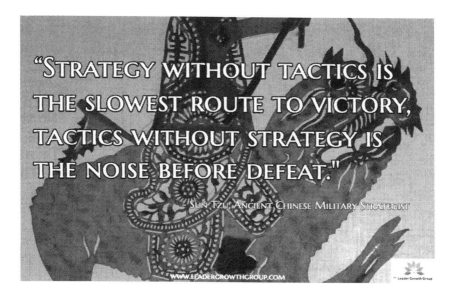

Execution is what translates ethereal strategy into tangible results. Yet, disciplined execution is a rarity in today's turbulent business environment. Learn to embody the three fundamentals of connection, adaptation, and collaboration...and all will marvel at your ability to get the mission accomplished!

Assess, Reflect, and Grow!

1. Self-Assess

⇒ How well do you know your strengths, weaknesses, and key stakeholder's needs?

1------------2-------------3-------------4-------------5-------------6-------------7
Not very well   I consistently revisit and assess

⇒ How well do you adapt to changing circumstances?

1------------2-------------3-------------4-------------5-------------6-------------7
I typically resist change   I am very flexible

⇒ How do you prefer to work?

1------------2-------------3-------------4-------------5-------------6-------------7
On my own   Collaborating with others

2. Reflect

⇒ Of the three "connections" for better execution, where can you improve as a leader?

_____
_____
_____
_____
_____

⇒ What are some ways you can cultivate a "beginner's mind" to increase adaptability?

_____
_____
_____
_____
_____
_____
_____

⇒ When do you contract as a leader and isolate yourself from collaboration opportunities?

_____
_____
_____
_____
_____
_____

3. Commit to New Growth

⇒ What is one simple thing (OST) you will do to help you practice one of these fundamentals of execution in your workplace?

_____
_____
_____
_____
_____
_____
_____

Leadership vs. Authority

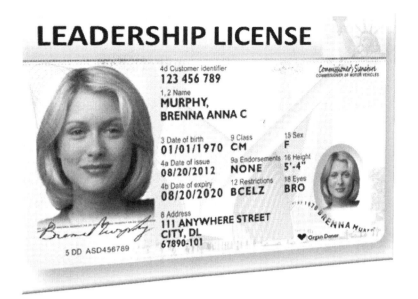

How to Get Your Leadership License

What if you could only be a leader in your organization if you first passed a leadership test? Consider something like getting your driver's license! Imagine this. On your big day, your proud mentor takes you to the Department of Leadership Certification (DLC). You are nervous as your number is called to enter a private booth and take a multiple-choice quiz on topics like emotional intelligence, teamwork, and leading organizations through change. You feel good about how things went, until your assessor calls for you to come and take your practical exam. You are then given a task and a team, and told to deliver results under challenging conditions. All the while, your assessor is scribbling notes on his clipboard about your performance. Hours later, you get your scores back…you've done it! You've passed your leadership test and earned your license to lead!

Sounds ridiculous, right? Well, as crazy as this may sound, many people out there are actually waiting for someone to "certify" them as a leader. They may not be formally taking a test; however, they are lingering until an authority deems them "worthy" of handling leadership responsibility. These are the people who tell themselves, "once I get that promotion, then I will be ready to lead." Or maybe it's, "once I get an M.B.A. from a prestigious institution, that's when I'll really start leading."

I've got a "secret" to share with you…No one can give you permission to lead; it's a choice you make all by yourself. It doesn't take a new title. It doesn't require an advanced degree. However, it does require you to see yourself as a leader. That's the real magic of getting recognized with a promotion or going through the ceremony of graduating from a credentialed program. These events change how we see ourselves. **When leadership becomes a part of your identity, one starts to embrace leadership behaviors more**. So, how do we flip the switch and start to see ourselves as leaders? Here are a few ideas:

1. Realize You Own the Power – Come on…Really?

Yes, really. Recognize that leadership is not about the title and has nothing to do with your credentials. Instead, these things often lend us authority. **Yet, authority is given to us whereas leadership is something you do all on your own.** If something in your organization 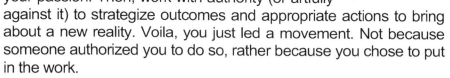 must change, begin with yourself first and model the change that's needed. Build your credibility and find others with shared values. Create strength through relational commitments and energize others through your passion. Then, work with authority (or artfully against it) to strategize outcomes and appropriate actions to bring about a new reality. Voila, you just led a movement. Not because someone authorized you to do so, rather because you chose to put in the work.

2. Practice Your Confidence – So why don't more

people put in the work required to lead? It's a combination of a few things. First, it's easier to <u>not</u> exercise leadership, and many just don't have the energy or determination within them. They would rather someone just do it for them. The second most common reason is people are afraid they might fail. They  say to themselves; "what if I put myself out there and nobody follows?" or "do I really have what it takes to make a difference?" There is only one way to know—give it a try. You build your confidence to lead by doing. Note also that it's often in failure we learn our greatest leadership lessons. Every time you step into the arena, you are building your leadership skills, and in the process, you gain confidence.

3. Be a Student of Leadership – The best leaders are insatiably curious and committed to life-long learning. They consistently pursue new knowledge and diverse perspectives on leadership. They read leadership books not only to gain fresh insights, but also to form their own opinions on what will work for them personally. They also try to surround themselves with other leaders and observe their behavior. Finally, they commit to their professional development. Whether it be signing up for a new training or working with an Executive Coach, they prepare themselves for the challenges of leadership.

The best leaders are simply the best learners, and life is their laboratory. Seek out discomfort, find support, and never stop growing.

www.leadergrowthgroup.com

If you haven't already bought into your own power to exhibit leadership, I hope this article has helped you to see things differently. If you know someone who has real potential to lead, yet hasn't created that identity for him or herself, please share this with them. With so many challenges today, the world need more leaders. Thankfully, we don't have to get a license to do so; we just need to choose to lead.

Assess, Reflect, and Grow!

1. Self-Assess

⇒ How much do you rely on formal authority when attempting to change something?

1------------2-------------3-------------4-------------5-------------6-------------7
It's imperative for leverage · It's my last resort

⇒ How do you personally prefer to develop your confidence?

1------------2-------------3-------------4-------------5-------------6-------------7
I act only if success is inevitable · · · · · · · · · · · · I do, fail, learn, & grow

⇒ How many leadership books do you read in a year?

1------------2-------------3-------------4-------------5-------------6-------------7
More like one every few years · · · · · · · · · · · · · · · · · · · Six or more

2. Reflect

⇒ In what types of situations do you give yourself permission to lead others?

_____

_____

_____

_____

_____

_____

⟹ When do you find yourself "not authorized" to take a leadership role?

_____
_____
_____
_____
_____
_____
_____

⟹ Where can you choose to lead and make a difference for others?

_____
_____
_____
_____
_____
_____
_____

3. Commit to New Growth

⟹ What is one simple thing (OST) you will do to create a mindset where you authorize yourself greater opportunity to exhibit leadership?

_____
_____
_____
_____
_____
_____
_____

"Soft Power" – Leading Without Authority

Have you ever tried leading a person or a group without any formal authority to fall back on? For many, this is one of the greatest leadership challenges we might face. Without the traditional "carrot or stick" to help get things done, we can feel powerless and limited in our ability to influence. Yet, some people seem to thrive in these situations and we admire their ability to still get things accomplished. I call this demonstration of applied emotional intelligence—leveraging "soft power." So, what are the secrets of "soft power" and how can we use it to accomplish both individual and team objectives? Here are three ideas to consider.

1. Give Power to Others - When working in groups where the formal power dynamics are flat, it is important to recognize that everyone is subconsciously "racking and stacking" one another and creating their own personal hierarchy. This evolutionary process is deeply ingrained within all humans and it has allowed us to organize ourselves for survival. Expect that there will be power plays as group members test to see where they fit in the group. **Instead** 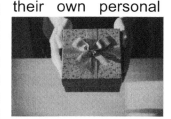 **of allowing these dynamics to naturally unfold, tactfully intervene and try to facilitate a space where everyone's voice gets heard.** Rather than leading with your opinion, ask for input from others and encourage quieter voices to speak up. Insist on mutual respect for all team members. In creating a space for power to be shared, others will trust in you more and naturally give you an informal leadership role.

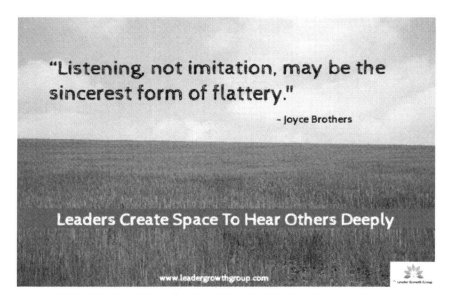

"Listening, not imitation, may be the sincerest form of flattery."

- Joyce Brothers

Leaders Create Space To Hear Others Deeply

www.leadergrowthgroup.com

2. Actively Listen - When we hold formal authority, we are frequently directing and telling others what needs to be done for the team to be successful. Thus, managers tend to get really good with their directing skills, often to the neglect of practicing their listening skills. **In a power flat relationship, it is the better listener who will assume leadership.** Use techniques like mirroring back what you heard and asking meaningful questions to gain further clarification. When others feel you are a great listener, they are more likely to trust you and, hence, give you referent power, which is the highest base of power a leader can access.

3. Serve & Synergize - In power flat relationships, the synergistic details that lead to better teamwork can often be

neglected as everyone stays in their personal lanes of responsibility. To be seen as a leader in a team, hunt down the resources that everyone knowingly needs, but no one finds the courage or the time to make a priority. Or perhaps you might seek out the management/stakeholder feedback needed to make the team work better, and then act as a liaison in making the team more aware. Make it your priority to help others succeed. **These small acts of service will increase your value to the team and others will intuitively begin to seek out your leadership**.

Leading a team without formal authority can often feel like a daunting challenge. Yet, when we smartly recognize the group dynamics at play and practice the use of "soft power," we provide the leadership necessary to achieve results. The next time you are leading without formal authority, try using some of the above ideas to influence others... you might be surprised at how persuasive you can become!

Assess, Reflect, and Grow!

1. Self-Assess

⟹ How skilled are you at creating space in a group for less powerful voices to be heard?

1------------2-------------3-------------4-------------5-------------6-------------7
I don't even think about it   I'm masterful at it

⟹ How well do you listen to others when engaged in a group conversation?

1------------2-------------3-------------4-------------5-------------6-------------7
I miss many key points   I track multiple threads concurrently

⟹ How well can you identify collective group needs that are going unmet?

1------------2-------------3-------------4-------------5-------------6-------------7
I am usually focused on my needs   I recognize group needs and act

2. Reflect

⟹ Where are there situations at work where you need to influence without authority?

_____

_____

_____

_____

_____

⇒ Given these situations identified above, what have you done to gain influence?

_____
_____
_____
_____
_____

⇒ What have you done to lose influence?

_____
_____
_____
_____
_____

⇒ Where are there unmet group needs that you might service?

_____
_____
_____
_____
_____

3. Commit to New Growth

⇒ What is one simple thing (OST) you will practice to increase your capacity for leadership when you hold little authority?

_____
_____
_____
_____
_____

What If We Have This Leadership Thing All Wrong?

Imagine that you just read an article on how your competition is steadily stealing your market share. This is nothing new to you. They have been out innovating you for some time now and it's now apparent that your current products or services are inferior. Slowly, you've seen your talent leave for greener pastures as rumors of downsizing abound. There is a fear permeating the organization as people wonder what the future holds. What's needed is a real leader! Someone who can come in and make things right again. We've seen this scenario play out time and again. The Board will likely remove the C-Suite and bring in a leadership savior. Yet, what if we have got this whole leadership thing all wrong? What if the very essence of how we define leadership is no longer serving us?

We can't really fault why we seek a leadership savior in these scenarios. It's ingrained in our DNA! *The Practice of Adaptive Leadership: Tools and Tactics for Changing Your Organization and the World* (Heifetz, Grashow, & Linsky, 2009) explains that since the dawn of time, we have engaged in a social contract within groups. Essentially, when a group member emerged to offer us much needed **direction, protection and order**, we in turn granted them **authority** over us.[3] As  long as this person kept their side of the bargain, we continued to reward them with increased power. At some point, we started calling this authority figure our Leader, Chief, or King, which anointed them with title and elevated social status as well. The key distinction to make here is that we started associating the exercising of authority with leadership. This is a huge mistake as leadership is totally different.

Given the above scenario, direction, protection and order is exactly what we crave. We want a new direction and our new leadership should have the ability to see what we cannot. We require protection from our competitors and the threat they present. We desire order as a power vacuum emerges from the loss of key talent. Yet, what if instead of providing the direction  we need to go, leadership helped us to figure out where we collectively want to go together? What if instead of sheltering us from our competitor's threats, leadership exposed the reality that we faced and challenged us to be more? What if instead of returning us to a calm and comfortable place, leadership taught us to embrace the chaos of change and to value living on the edge of constant learning? In short, what might happen if instead of exercising authority, our leadership actually **led** us?

WHEN SAILING THE SEAS OF UNCERTAINTY, LEADERS PROVIDE THE CREW WITH VISION BEYOND THE HORIZON AND THE PRINCIPLES BY WHICH THEY MUST NAVIGATE TO STAY THE COURSE.

www.leadergrowthgroup.com

Intuitively, we get this. While management is an important aspect of a productive society, deep down inside, we all want to be led more so than managed. When we experience true leadership, we feel empowered to grow to our full potential. Outside of experiencing love, there is perhaps no greater feeling than pushing yourself to be more than you thought you could be. Yet, with the pleasure of growth, we often experience loss and pain. We must let go of a part of ourselves to create the space for learning something new. Learning then becomes a series of failures until we ultimately get it right. This can be a very disappointing and humbling process. **Thus, true leadership requires us to disappoint our followers at a rate that they can tolerate[4].**

This is the very reason why we see more authority rather than leadership being exercised in our world. There is a real art to establishing enough trust with followers so that they allow you to disappoint them. Disappoint them too much and you will soon be looking for a new job. Yet, it's important to note that if you disappoint them too little, as when exercising pure authority, you will also be looking for a new job! Exercising authority

will not promote the learning needed for organizational growth, and, thus, results will be the same over time. With consistently poor to average results, you will eventually be replaced as your organization seeks out new "leadership."

Therefore, the next time you feel the pull to provide direction, protection and order to your team, take a step back and try to recognize what is really needed in this moment. Start **practicing leadership rather than exercising authority** and watch your organization begin to flourish.

Assess, Reflect, and Grow!

1. Self-Assess

⇒ What do find yourself doing most often with your team?

1------------2-------------3-------------4-------------5-------------6------------7
Providing protection, direction, and order   Leading change

⇒ How comfortable are you as a leader with disappointing your followers?

1------------2-------------3-------------4-------------5-------------6------------7
No way! I'm a people pleaser   No problem! It's part of my role

⇒ How politically savvy are you as a leader?

1------------2-------------3-------------4-------------5-------------6------------7
I don't play politics   I use politics to my advantage

2. Reflect

⇒ When does your team expect you to fulfill the role of an authority figure?

_____

_____

_____

_____

_____

_____

⇒ When does it serve your team to not tell them what they want to hear?

_____

_____

_____

_____

_____

⇒ Where does your team need you to challenge them to learn and grow?

_____

_____

_____

_____

_____

⇒ Learning new things can be painful...how much can your team tolerate right now?

_____

_____

_____

_____

_____

3. Commit to New Growth

⇒ What is one simple thing (OST) you will practice to "disappoint followers at a rate they can tolerate" so that new learning and growth can occur?

_____

_____

_____

_____

Motivating Performance and Change

David Spungin

Google's Surprising Insights on Team Effectiveness

After two plus years of rigorous research leveraging over 200 interviews focused on 250 attributes of 180 active teams, Google's People Operations (think HR department with analytics capabilities) determined there is one question that every leader should be asking themselves if they are seeking to create an effective team...

How's our psychological safety coming along?

Huh? Yes, I had the same reaction when I first read the research. You mean to tell me that building an effective team is not about selecting the right mix of talented people who possess unique skillsets that complement one another? Or that forming effective teams is not mostly about creating "team chemistry," and aligning personality traits to where team members gel together naturally. Nope. **Apparently, it's not so much about <u>who</u> is on** the team, but more about <u>how</u> people interact with each other[5]. While Google's researchers discovered five key findings that set its best teams apart from others, psychological safety was clearly the most important...and the more you read about it, the more sense it makes.

So, what is psychological safety and how can we know if it exists within our team? The short answer is that psychological safety is the underpinnings that lead to a trusting environment. Do you feel safe with your fellow team members? Are they willing to both challenge and support you in a positive manner? Do they have your best interests at heart? Will they listen empathetically to your ideas and in a non-judgmental way? Can you be vulnerable with one another, to include sharing each other's mistakes and shortcomings? These are just a few questions that one can use to assess the level of psychological safety within their team.

This is related to what we know from recent brain-based research, in that we as human beings have a need for status and relatedness[6]. When we come together as a team, we are constantly assessing where we stand within the team's "pecking order" and if we are a part of the "in" or "out" group. This causes us to be guarded in our interactions and limits our willingness to take risks with one another. We simply don't want others to negatively assess our "competence, awareness, or positivity."[7] Perhaps more importantly, "in the absence of safe social interactions, the body generates a threat response."[8] When our bodies become inundated with cortisol and testosterone, and are focused on how to either fight against or flee from fellow team members, we can assume that trust will be degraded.

So, what can a leader do to create the conditions for greater psychological safety to exist on their team? Here are a few ideas to consider:

1. Communicate Expectations – If you are leading a group and have formal authority as well, **be clear and upfront with how you would like team members to interact with one another**. For example, expressing, "Team, I want you to  know that I truly value everyone's opinion, and, as such, I expect that you will bring your ideas forward, no matter how crazy they may sound or how contradictory they may be. Furthermore, this is a safe space to do so and I will not tolerate personal attacks in our interactions. We want to challenge each other and foster healthy debate, but not at the expense of our relationships. Can we agree to this?" If you are attempting to influence a team without formal authority, you might make a similar offer and then work towards norms that will allow for peer accountability and enforcement.

2. Be the Example – A leader is always on a stage and team members are constantly looking to the leader and determining "what right looks like" in how they will interact with one another. If you as a leader are not present, not fully listening, discounting others' ideas, interrupting, or ignoring certain voices…others will undoubtedly do the same. So, after you clearly set expectations, work hard to model those expectations and give team members license to call you out if you are not! **Perhaps the most important area where a leader needs to lead by example is in expressing vulnerability**. If you don't offer your shortcomings and mistakes to the group first, don't expect anyone to let down their defenses either.

A leader is always on a stage. Every action or inaction is teaching followers what is acceptable and what is not within the team's culture.

www.leadergrowthgroup.com

3. Lead Through Facilitation – A team's culture will
not only be shaped by the leader's behavior, but also by what
behavior he or she allows from others. A wise leader will practice
upholding shared values and facilitating productive conversation.
When an unfair interruption has occurred, someone might say,
"wait a second, Jim, let's hear out what Jane was just saying and
we'll come back to you once she's finished." If a team member
has been noticeably quiet, the leader may practice inclusiveness
by saying, "Pranov, we haven't heard from you yet; please help
us to understand your stance on the
issue." If the team is dealing with a failure
and assigning blame to each other, the
leader may offer, "we all had a role to play
in this, including myself. I want us to stop
focusing on who is to blame and start
focusing on what we have learned and how we can solve the
problem." **The foundation of good facilitation is curiosity**.
Always be asking yourself, what's most important right now and
what questions or statements will help move the team forward
together?

Google's latest research on teams helped to confirm what
many of us already knew, **without trust, there can be no
team**. And while the term psychological safety may be new to
us, we all intuitively get it — people need to feel safe with each
other to trust one another. The real value in this work is in
helping leaders to identify where they need to focus their efforts
in creating the conditions for psychological safety to exist.
Thus, I offer that you reflect upon your own team....**How's
your psychological safety coming along?**

Assess, Reflect, and Grow!

1. Self-Assess

⇒ Have you clearly communicated expectations for how team members should interact?

1-----------2------------3------------4------------5------------6------------7
No, didn't think I needed to   Yes, and we consistently revisit them

⇒ How likely are team members to "call you out" if you are not setting a good example?

1-----------2------------3------------4------------5------------6------------7
I'm their boss, that's disrespectful   They do it often, and I appreciate it!

⇒ How practiced are you at using facilitation to uphold group communication standards?

1-----------2------------3------------4------------5------------6------------7
I've never tried it   I facilitate standards everyday

2. Reflect

⇒ How likely are team members to challenge your perspective in decision-making?

_____

_____

_____

_____

_____

⇒ What's the standard for interrupting one another on your team?

_____

_____

_____

_____

_____

⇒ Who gets heard most often in your team...who gets heard least often?

_____

_____

_____

_____

_____

_____

⇒ How likely are team members to take risks with one another?

_____

_____

_____

_____

_____

_____

3. Commit to New Growth

⇒ What is one simple thing (OST) you will practice to increase your team's effectiveness?

_____

_____

_____

_____

_____

_____

The Leadership Equation

Part of West Point's academic curriculum requires every cadet to study the natural sciences, advanced mathematics classes, and an engineering discipline of choice. While I often struggled in these challenging courses as a cadet, it was likely here that I developed my fondness for logic and a healthy respect for a sound equation. A well proven equation really is a thing of beauty. In a concise set of symbols, one can communicate volumes of information and help to explain the world around us. For example, Einstein's mass-energy equivalence equation ($E=mc^2$) is considered pure genius because it unlocked one of the greatest mysteries of the universe in just five simple characters. I share this with you because equations can similarly help us to explain the inner workings of organizational life and help develop us as leaders.

In fact, there is one equation that continuously guides me as a Leadership Development professional. It stems from the work of organizational development scholar & practitioner, Kurt Lewin, and is as relevant today as when he first theorized it back in 1943. While not an actual mathematical equation representing quantifiable relationships, it is a heuristic formula that accurately explains one of the biggest challenges of leadership and it's as simple as this:

$$B = f(P, E)$$

Lewin's formula states that behavior (B) is a function (f) of the person (P) and his or her environment (E). Thus, if you are seeking to change an individual's behavior, you must influence one of two variables (or preferably both for maximum effect). Leadership, at its heart, is often about moving individuals and organizations through change and Lewin's formula gives us a practical way of organizing our efforts. Looking at your own team as an example, perhaps there are behavioral tendencies that are negatively impacting performance and you would like to see change for the better. Let's first work with the idea of shifting behavior by focusing on the individual person.

It's important to note that you can never really change another person, they must change themselves. Attempting to force behavioral change on another individual is likely to incite resistance and is ultimately unsustainable. Yet, often, this is the norm as managers leverage their proverbial carrots and sticks to shape organizational outcomes. The real leadership challenge at hand is the appropriate way to inspire an individual to want to learn to behave differently and better align with the team's goals. Well, much of that inspirational ability stems from your own behavior and example as a leader. Are you a person of character, competence, and credibility? Are you demonstrating an authentic empathy with those you are leading? Do you own your vulnerabilities and have you established a track record of personal accountability? These are just some of the leadership behaviors that are a prerequisite for inspiring another person to change their behavior. **It comes down to this — do followers admire and respect you enough as a leader to make the difficult process of changing themselves an imperative?**

Now let's look at how the environment impacts behavior and performance outcomes. Are your team's behavioral challenges

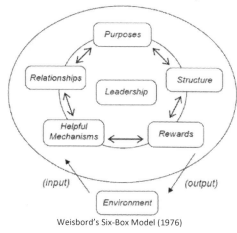

Weisbord's Six-Box Model (1976)

isolated to a few individuals or is there evidence of a systemic issue? If the latter is true, exercising leadership now becomes more about addressing environmental factors like values, mission, vision, structure, relationships, technologies, and reward mechanisms that are not producing the desired behavior. Perhaps your organization's structure is fostering competition over collaboration and promoting selfishness. Or maybe there is a values-disconnect between what executives are communicating as the priority and what front line workers are expected to deliver on.

Whatever the environmental challenge, the savvy leader understands that changing the organization's environment is a much larger undertaking and should be approached with caution. **There is risk in championing change as every system is perfectly designed to produce the results it gets.** There will undoubtedly be stakeholders that have a vested interest in keeping things exactly how they are. One will need to build a strong case for change and create alliances with organizational authority that can help generate movement.

In summary, the B=f(P,E) formula gives us a simple yet powerful way to determine things we can do to improve individual, team and organizational performance. **Leadership is about facilitating change and behavior is how we can tangibly interpret progress towards desired change.** When seeking to move the needle in a positive direction, a leader can look to influence the individual directly and/or seek to shift environmental factors that are impacting outcomes. Regardless of the point of influence you choose, it's essential that you are personally practicing the leadership behaviors you are seeking from others. No individual or system will adopt your vision for change if they do not see you first being the example.

Assess, Reflect, and Grow!

1. Self-Assess

⇒ When you provide constructive feedback to others, do people admire and respect you enough to change themselves?

1------------2-------------3-------------4-------------5-------------6-------------7
I usually must keep after them   Yes, my opinion can shift people

⇒ How well do values, mission, and vision reinforce desired behavior in your organization?

1------------2-------------3-------------4-------------5-------------6-------------7
We are utterly out of alignment   We have absolute synergy

⇒ How well do structure, relationships, technologies, and reward mechanisms reinforce desired behavior in your organization?

1------------2-------------3-------------4-------------5-------------6-------------7
We are utterly out of alignment   We have absolute synergy

2. Reflect

⇒ What results is your organization perfectly designed to produce?

_____

_____

_____

_____

_____

_____

⇒ Think of someone who is not performing on your team...how does this person's behavior need to change for them to become more effective?

_____

_____

_____

_____

_____

_____

⇒ Given how this person needs to change him or herself...How could the organizational environment change to inspire desired behavior and curtail ineffective behavior?

_____

_____

_____

_____

_____

_____

3. Commit to New Growth

⇒ What is one simple thing (OST) you will do to more effectively shape the desired behavior you'd like to see from team members?

_____

_____

_____

_____

_____

_____

_____

Engineering Effective Change

Imagine you are a manager in a software engineering firm. You're a smart and practical problem solver who inspires trust in your team. All is going smoothly until one day you realize the need to promote or reassign a few team members. Or maybe it's something more substantial like implementing a new information technology system. No problem! You will handle this like any other challenge you face: acquiring data, analyzing options, designing solutions, and, finally, implementing the change. It all seems logical and you are confident the process will yield success. Then it doesn't. In fact, you encounter stiff resistance as people drag their feet to adopt your change initiative. What happened? Truth be told...this was a very predictable outcome.

More than 70% of organizational change efforts FAIL!

You might find it comforting to know that you are not alone, as more than 70% of all organizational change efforts fail. While these failures occur for many reasons, consistent themes include **attempting to solve adaptive challenges through technical problem solving** and the common **assumption that change can be managed** to fruition. Technical professionals often embrace these conventions when attempting to manifest change as they tend to value linear and systematic processes that enable a sense of control. Yet, changing human systems is habitually messy and unpredictable by nature. Is it realistic to think that a formulaic change process might work? An analytically minded person myself, I have struggled with this question for years. My conclusion is that while a prescribed change framework might not be feasible, there are several key principles that every change agent should consider. Specifically, one must be mindful of: **1) Preparing the system for change, 2) Initiating the change using "soft energy", and 3) Sustaining the change through "hard energy."**

Preparing a system for change is an often overlooked but critical change principle. Before engaging in change, one needs to understand where the system is starting from. What is the current state? Who are the key stakeholders? How might cultural norms and belief systems impact a proposed change? What is the perceived  sense of urgency for change? These are just a few of the questions – leaders must ask themselves. Yet, perhaps the most important preparatory question is, "who stands to lose the most from this change?" **People don't resist change, they resist loss**. In particular, those who believe they may lose power and influence are the ones most likely to resist. Having thought through these questions and developed a compelling case for change, the savvy change agent will then secure buy-in from the highest sources of power in the system. Executive support helps in generating key alliances and centers of power to move the system in the desired direction.

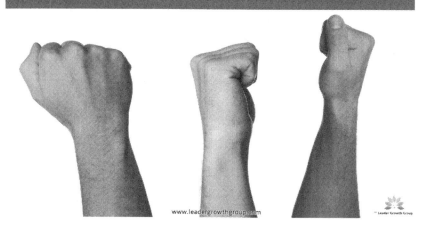

Now that you have organizational muscle behind you, do the unexpected. Rather than imposing your change plan on the system, initiate the change by using "soft energy." **Soft energy is about acknowledging the difficulty of change and disrupting compassionately**. This is also the energy of possibilities and emergence. Start by inviting all the key stakeholders into the change conversation and give them a voice. This process is often messy and unscripted. Facilitate the conversation and avoid directing it, while allowing for needs and concerns to be heard. Control must be abandoned in favor of faith. **The more the group owns the change process, the more likely they are to act**. Soft energy also  means understanding that change creates anxiety in the system and your role as the change agent should be to transform that angst. This is often accomplished by **helping the system transition from fear to curiosity**. Once a plan for change is agreed upon, constant and transparent communication of the vision is imperative for transformation to occur. When people "see" where they are going, they feel more in control and less anxious.

Finally, soft energy is not enough, we also must implement a "hard energy" if we desire sustained change. **Hard energy is challenging, focused, calculated, and persistent**. This is the  energy of driving towards closure. This does not mean that we forcefully coerce the system to change; rather this is about **avoiding distractions and measuring performance**. Organizations are what they measure and the same principle applies to a change initiative. Thus, identify the metrics associated with change success early and monitor progress. Challenge the system to meet goals and objectives while utilizing social pressure to pull the organization forward. Finally, reward early adopters accordingly and share examples of group success whenever possible.

While there may not be a way to truly "engineer" effective change, there are key principles that can increase your chances for change success. By first preparing the system for change, one ensures an understanding of the politics, potential losses, and centers of power needed to generate momentum. By initiating the change through use of soft energy, one disarms opponents with empathy and involves the system in determining its own solution. By using hard energy, one helps the group stay focused and on track as it embodies the change over time. I invite you to master these tools of organizational change and lead your team to new heights of achievement.

Assess, Reflect, and Grow!

1. Self-Assess

⇒ When initiating a change effort, how thoroughly do you map potential losses for others?

1-----------2-------------3------------4------------5------------6------------7
Surface level understanding   I deeply grasp losses of power & influence

⇒ When initiating a change effort, do you involve others in the decision-making?

1-----------2-------------3------------4------------5------------6------------7
No, I like to create the plan myself   Absolutely, to the lowest level possible

⇒ When implementing a change effort, do you get distracted from your intended goals?

1-----------2-------------3------------4------------5------------6------------7
Often, I rarely accomplish my intent   Never! I am laser-like focused

2. Reflect

⇒ Where in your organization are managers trying to apply technical problem solving to human systems challenges?

_____

_____

_____

_____

_____

⇒ If you could change anything in your organization, what would it be? If you were to implement something new, who stands to lose the most?

_____

_____

_____

_____

_____

_____

⇒ If you were to implement something new, how could you disrupt compassionately? What outcomes would you measure to ensure you stayed on track?

_____

_____

_____

_____

_____

_____

3. Commit to New Growth

⇒ What is one simple thing (OST) you will do to practice becoming a more powerful change agent within your organization?

_____

_____

_____

_____

_____

_____

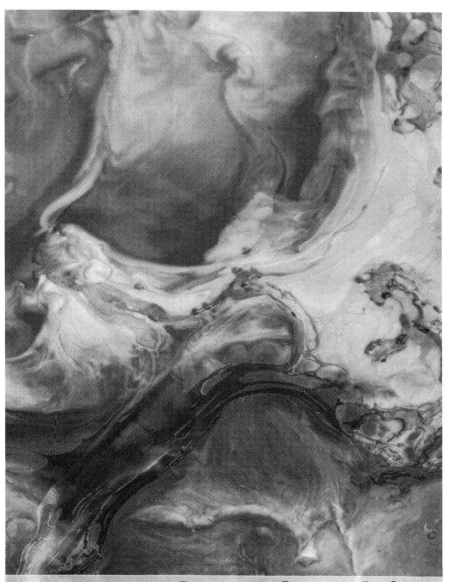

Creative Leadership
Lessons

3 Leadership Lessons from Dr. Seuss

Many of you may not know this about me, but I have four young kids ranging from one to ten years old. As a family, we enjoy reading a lot of children's books together and over the years, we've determined a few favorites. At the top of our list are several books written by Dr. Seuss. His rhymes are fun to read, and the brightly colored illustrations capture their imagination. I've also noticed that some of his stories carry a wonderful leadership message within them. A message that many adults could stand to revisit. Here are three of my favorites:

"You hush your mouth!" howled the mighty King Yertle.

"You've got no right to talk to the world's highest turtle.

I rule from the clouds! Over Land! Over sea!

There's nothing, no, NOTHING, that's higher than me!"[9]

Dr. Seuss stated that King Yertle represented Adolf Hitler

118

1. *Yertle the Turtle* – These are King Yertle's famous last words. Just a few pages later, we find him falling from his great height, face first in the mud, never to rule again. How did the once proud and mighty king end up like this? Well, he wasn't grateful for the wonderful kingdom he already had and became overly ambitious. Leveraging his positional power for his personal benefit, he literally walks on the backs of his subordinates to make himself more magnificent. Meanwhile, he treats his people with great disrespect. If you've been in the workforce for more than a day, you have probably met your own personal Yertle somewhere in your career. **Leadership lesson…don't be King Yertle! Instead, embrace humility as a leader and use your power to serve, rather than exploit, others.**

But, because they had stars, all the Star-Belly Sneetches
Would brag, "We're the best kind of Sneetch on the beaches."
With their snoots in the air, they would sniff and they'd snort
"We'll have nothing to do with the Plain-Belly sort!"[10]

Photo by theilr via flickr

2. *The Sneetches* – Oh, those silly Sneetches! Always trying to outdo one another and put down those that are not like them. There are several solid lessons here. In the formation of all groups, a natural phenomenon unfolds where "racking and stacking" takes place. We are unconsciously determining the social pecking order, and this often results with an "in-group" and an "out-group." When this occurs, unspoken jealousy and resentment can plague a team's dynamics and effectiveness. **Leadership lesson…no kind of Sneetch is the best on the beaches! All team members have unique value. Leaders must be aware of where unhealthy dynamics are festering in their team and learn to unleash the often-repressed value that the "out-group" brings through their diversity.**

Then the North-Going Zax

puffed his chest up with pride.

"I never," take a step to one side.

And I'll prove to you that I won't change my ways

If I have to keep standing here fifty-nine days!"[11]

3. The Zax – *This one is my favorite! It's a short tale of two prideful and stubborn Zax who find themselves at a crossroads, unable to compromise on a solution (great metaphor for the current state of American politics, anyone?). Instead of exercising empathy and compassion, the two Zax angrily argue their individual viewpoints. The result—zero progress and personal irrelevance as the world passes them by.* **Leadership lesson...learn to notice your inner Zax and manage it accordingly. Leaders should be principled and passionate, however, not to where they are getting in their own way.**

Author's Note - If you enjoyed this article and have kids, you might also enjoy my children's book, "The Legend of Stinky Toes McGee.**" Inspired by Dr. Seuss, it's intended to teach kids that some problems cannot be solved with our heads, but rather, they can only be solved with our hearts. You can pick up a paperback or digital copy exclusively on Amazon.*

Assess, Reflect, and Grow!

1. Self-Assess

⇒ How would you assess the level of humility you exhibit as a leader?

1-----------2-------------3------------4------------5------------6------------7
None! Leaders must be bold   It's hard to even rate myself a 7

⇒ How important do you think it is for a leader to be inclusive?

1-----------2-------------3------------4------------5------------6------------7
Either you fit in or you don't   Diversity and inclusiveness is a top priority

⇒ How inclined are you to "get in your own way" when debating an opinion?

1-----------2-------------3------------4------------5------------6------------7
It happens all the time   Never! I realize when I am becoming ineffective

2. Reflect

⇒ Which of these leadership lessons from Dr. Seuss most resonates with you and why?

_____

_____

_____

_____

_____

_____

⇒ Where on your team are there people who feel like they are an outsider? What could you do to make them feel more they are a part of the team?

_____

_____

_____

_____

_____

_____

⇒ When might your "inner Zax" show up for you? What situations for you trigger stubbornness or arrogance?

_____

_____

_____

_____

_____

_____

3. Commit to New Growth

⇒ Given these simple but powerful lessons/reminders, what is one simple thing (OST) you will do to practice better leadership?

_____

_____

_____

_____

_____

_____

_____

_____

Can a Llama Teach You Leadership?

Photo Credit: Mike Lerario

Having finished cinching down the buckles of our llama's saddle, my tent mates and I took turns loading our gear on the animal for the first time. It was a hot day and we were sweating greatly, yet as my eyes shifted to the trail ahead, it was clear the snow-capped peaks in the distance would offer something quite different. I am part of a National Outdoor Leadership School (NOLS) expedition where a

group of thirteen senior executives are practicing the art of leadership by exploring the Wyoming backcountry together. We will navigate many miles of increasing elevation daily. We will learn new outdoor skills and how to care for the environment. Yet, most importantly, we will learn to behave in ways that inspire deep trust with one another.

A core part of the learning comes from the llamas themselves. Magnificently agile animals, they can leap over three feet high logs, with 70 pounds on their backs, and calmly stick the landing on the side of a wet cliff. It's an amazing sight to behold. And much like humans, they also have different personalities, varying moods and preferences. Some are more dominant than others and "act up" if placed in the back of the pack. Others are almost cliquey in nature, and will only move efficiently when placed next to their best bud.

Similar to leading with a team of direct reports toward a goal, our group had to learn how the llamas wanted to be managed! We had to uncover the pack's dynamics, assess their personal needs, and then adjust our management style to meet those needs. For instance, we quickly learned that a command and control style would often backfire immediately (as it does in most modern organizations). In fact, push too hard, and you just might get spit on in retaliation! However (unless you speak llama) it's rather hard to communicate a vision and then empower a llama to drive results. The llamas needed a balanced approach to leadership; not only one that considered the environmental pressures being placed on us to accomplish the day's mission, but also brought them into the decision-making process. Over the course of seven days together, here's what a bunch of llamas taught us:

1. Know when to give 'em more lead, and when to reel 'em in - We all took turns as a llama handler as we trekked across the remote and sometimes dangerous terrain. When guiding your animal, you hold on to what's called a lead, which attaches to their bridle and gives you about 6 feet of rope

 to work with. Mastering how much of that lead you hold in your hands is an art and it's constantly changing. When navigating tight areas, you might shorten it to just a foot or two so you maintain strong control. When crossing a fast-moving creek, you might release all the length,

giving your llama the freedom to cross the danger as he sees best. The parallels to leading a direct report are clear. Sometimes, they "don't know what they don't know," and you need to provide strong direction and guidance to best help them. Other times, strong guidance works against you as a manager, and reports need space to find their own solutions. **A great manager does not adopt a single style of leadership, rather applies the right style based on the individual's need and the task at hand.**

2. Listen to your llama, sometimes they know best -

On day five, we began our descent from roughly 11,500 feet. The terrain was steep, rocky, and the riskiest part of the week's expedition. As we descended, it was unclear as to where a

proper trail was at times. At one point, we attempted to lead our llamas down a particularly steep part of the trail. We knew it wasn't a great route, but it looked doable and appeared to be our only option. Then our lead llama just stopped in his tracks. "Not going that way," he communicated to us by digging his heels in and refusing to budge another step. At first, we tried pulling harder, then we tried a gentle smack to the animal's rear. Usually, this would get your llama moving again, but this time, it was different. He just sat there, looking at us like we were crazy. Then it occurred to us, maybe he knows something we don't and we started searching harder for an alternate route. Lo and behold, there was a much better trail about 20 feet to our left! The llamas then followed us down safely. The lesson was clear, **sometimes as a leader, you must get out of your own way**. **There will be times when your followers know best**. Perhaps it's the front-line manager who knows your customer's needs better than you do. Or maybe it's the brilliant middle manager who just needs space to voice that next best idea to the company. **The best managers know when to lead and when to follow**.

3. Love your llama, and your llama will love you back -

Finally, the llamas helped ground the importance of being a servant leader. When you are deep in the backcountry, you quickly realize how important the llamas really are. If one were to get injured or developed a saddle sore, we as a team would be carrying an additional 70 pounds between us. As such, we used an old cavalry  saying to help guide our priorities of work each day; *"First, take care of the horse, then the saddle, then the man."* This translated to first feeding and watering your llama, then setting up your group's tent and collective responsibilities, then tending to all your personal needs. Repeating this process multiple times a day emphasized where a leader needs to be dedicating his or her valuable time. You simply won't meet your goals without your follower's dedication and team's support. Yet, when your actions consistently demonstrate a willingness to put other's needs above your own, you cannot fail to inspire respect, admiration and loyalty.

So yes, I believe that you <u>can</u> learn much about leadership from a llama. In fact, the greatest lessons often came from <u>allowing</u> a llama to lead you. Yet, like all successful relationships, it is a reciprocal dance of "give and take." The llamas would be lost without us, wandering aimlessly without purpose, and we lost without them, struggling mightily under the limits of our human capacities. I offer that you go find those llamas in your life that need your leadership, then **practice working the lead, listening deeply when challenged, and serving them every da**y. Do so, and you are destined to climb some impressive mountains together.

Assess, Reflect, and Grow!

1. Self-Assess

⇒ How flexible is your leadership style?

1------------2-------------3-------------4-------------5-------------6-------------7
I have one solid leadership style   I change styles to meet other's needs

⇒ How comfortable are you with having experts on your team that know more than you?

1------------2-------------3-------------4-------------5-------------6-------------7
It drives me crazy. I like to be in control!   It makes us better. I lean into them!

⇒ Think critically...how much of your day is spent serving your needs vs. others' needs?

1------------2-------------3-------------4-------------5-------------6-------------7
Honestly, my needs come first   I always serve others before self

2. Reflect

⇒ Describe your default leadership style in a few words? With what types of people is that style effective? With what types of personalities does your style not work well?

_____

_____

_____

_____

_____

⇒ Where are there opportunities for you to rely on other's expertise and release decision-making authority to them?

_____

_____

_____

_____

_____

_____

_____

⇒ Where are there opportunities to be more of a servant leader to your team?

_____

_____

_____

_____

_____

_____

_____

3. Commit to New Growth

⇒ Given this article's lessons, what is one simple thing (OST) you will do to practice better leadership?

_____

_____

_____

_____

_____

_____

_____

8 Songs That Can Teach You Leadership

Have you ever wondered why you can easily remember the lyrics to a catchy song from years ago, yet find it hard to recall what you ate just yesterday for breakfast? Music has an uncanny ability to circumvent our logical brains and instead lives deeply within our emotional bodies. When we resonate with a powerful tune or are inspired by a musician's message, we can instantly recall how it made us feel. This has me thinking about the real power of music and what this medium might offer in terms of learning leadership. Curious as to what lessons my own meager collection (about 5K tracks on my iTunes) might ascertain, I recently re-listened to a few favorites, but with my "leadership headphones" on….this is what I heard:

1. **Man in the Mirror** *by Michael Jackson*

"I'm starting with the man in the mirror

I'm asking him to change his ways

And no message could have been any clearer

If you want to make the world a better place

Take a look at yourself, and then make a change"

The King of Pop was on to something here. Every leader must learn to lead him or herself first. This often means having the courage to realize when you're ineffective and what adjustments you might need to make. As leaders, we are always changing, as are the environments in which we lead. **Constant self-assessment and feedback are critical to understanding that man (or woman) in the mirror**. The best leaders make this a consistent practice in their lives.

2. **I'm Not Afraid** *by Eminem*

"I'm not afraid, to take a stand

Everybody, come take my hand

We'll walk this road together, through the storm

Whatever weather, cold or warm

Just letting you know that you're not alone

Holler if you feel like you've been down the same road"

While Eminem might be far from your idea of a model leader, in "I'm Not Afraid," a more mature voice emerges as he raps about the struggles of overcoming drug/alcohol addiction and fully owning his responsibilities as a parent. The main chorus elicits a theme that is reoccurring in many of his songs — I understand your pain, I am willing to sacrifice for you, join me and together we shall overcome. This is the same call to action that every leader must make if they are to recruit and maintain followers. **Great leaders communicate their empathy for follower's needs, embody a philosophy of selfless-service, and align the team in a common purpose.**

3. **Imagine** *by John Lennon*

"Imagine no possessions

I wonder if you can

No need for greed or hunger

A brotherhood of man

Imagine all the people

Sharing all the world"

In this celebrated song, John Lennon asks the listener to imagine a world freed from class, religious, or political boundaries. He also encourages people to focus less on material possessions. Ultimately, the song is a passionate call for world peace. Could there be a better example of how to create and express a vision? Lennon does a masterful job of **understanding the current situation** (written in 1971 during the Vietnam War), **envisioning a different future, and communicating a path in a succinct and powerful way that challenges others to act**. The real testament to his genius is that his call for more tolerance and equality is no less relevant today.

4. **This is not a Song it's an Outburst: The Establishment Blues** *by Rodriguez*

"This system's gonna fall soon

To an angry young tune

And that's, a concrete cold fact"

If you don't yet know the story of Rodriquez, I highly recommend you watch the award winning documentary on his life and music, "*Searching For Sugar Man.*" Early in Rodriquez's career, he wrote a powerful tune called, "*This is not a Song it's an Outburst: The Establishment Blues.*" It was a call to action that no one heard in the United States. It sold very little copies and Rodriguez's career essentially flopped. Yet, years later, the song became an anthem for South Africans to revolt against the evil of Apartheid and sold millions of records. The leadership message is clear. **Not everyone is fit to lead in every environment. Hone your abilities, hold to your values, and practice authentically bringing your leadership gifts to the world**. Ultimately, with enough patience, those who need your leadership most will find you.

5. **Get Up Stand Up** *by Bob Marley*

"Get up, stand up, stand up for your right

Get up, stand up, don't give up the fight

Get up, stand up. Life is your right

So we can't give up the fight"

This iconic reggae song was conceived while Marley was touring Haiti. He was so extremely moved both by the lives of the Haitians and the extreme poverty they faced; that he called for all to "Get Up Stand Up" and fight for greater equality in the world. Leadership is often about fighting the status quo, and sustaining yourself in such battles requires tremendous energy. This can be difficult to sustain over time. **A leader who cannot passionately advocate for a mission will never attract and retain followers. Thus, wise leaders prudently take on the issues that give them a strongest sense of meaning and purpose.** Figure out what makes you "Get Up Stand Up" and lead the change you most desire.

6. **Tough** *by Craig Morgan*

"She's strong, pushes on, can't slow her down

She can take anything life dishes out

There was a time

Back before she was mine

When I thought I was tough"

In Western corporate culture, there can be a tendency to overly value the warrior/hero archetype of leadership and then falsely attribute those qualities more frequently to men. Craig Morgan's country hit, "Tough" reminds us that real toughness, like leadership, can come from anywhere. The warrior/hero in this song is his wife who manages the challenges of their day-to day lives with ease. Then when she struggles through a bout with cancer, he marvels at her will and resiliency. Leaders should be mindful of their own assessments of what a leader is and isn't. **Know that leadership can come from anyone in your organization and make a point to recognize the often-overlooked leadership that is being exhibited all around you.**

7. **Blue Train** *by John Coltrane*

No Lyrics...All instrumental bliss.

A portrait of John Coltrane
by Paolo Steffan, 2007

Pretty much any classic jazz track would suffice here, I chose Coltrane's "Blue Train" for its mix of catchy riffs and universal appeal. Rather than providing a message that relates to leadership, performing Jazz in itself is an act of leadership. In fact, leadership guru, Max DePree, wrote a book about the links between jazz and leadership called "Leadership Jazz" back in 1993 (Leadership Jazz). In essence, DePree writes that leaders, like jazz musicians, must stay attuned to the needs and ideas of their followers and even step aside at times to be followers themselves. Listen to "Blue Train" and you can hear this philosophy come to light. Coltrane asserts himself when appropriate while also bringing out the best in those around him. It's masterful.

8. **Staying Alive** *by The Bee Gees*

"Whether you're a brother or whether you're a mother,

You're stayin' alive, stayin' alive.

Feel the city breakin' and everybody shakin',

And we're stayin' alive, stayin' alive.

Ah, ha, ha, ha, stayin' alive, stayin' alive."

What could the Bee Gees possibly teach us about leadership you might ask? While their 1977 Grammy award winning hit might not have been intended to have anything to do with leadership — it might as well be every true leader's personal anthem. Whenever you choose to exhibit leadership, you are moving against a norm and often against authority whose job it is to maintain those norms. Move too fast or without proper support and you're likely to experience what Harvard Leadership professors, Ron Heifetz and Marty Linsky, call "getting assassinated" (a.k.a. getting fired or marginalized to the extent where you are no longer effective). Surfacing conflict and challenging the status quo will cause people to experience pain. Savvy leaders understand this and raise and lower the heat accordingly, moving the needle while simultaneously keeping themselves in the game. Leadership is risky business and it's all about staying alive!

So, there you have it. Eight songs that will hopefully inspire you to think about your own leadership and how you can be more effective as a leader. I also realize this list is far from all-encompassing, so if you have a favorite to add, I'd love to hear from you!

Author's Note — Since this article was first published in November 2014 on LinkedIn, it has received over 50K views (at time of this writing). Many people have chimed in and offered songs that might have made their list. It's also been pointed out that the list does not include a female artist. While unintentional, this is an unfortunate oversight on my part. Help me out! If you have suggestions, I would sincerely appreciate your thoughts for an all female artist follow-up article.

Assess, Reflect, and Grow!

1. Self-Assess

⇒ How well do you communicate other's pain points in your organization?

1------------2-------------3-------------4-------------5-------------6-------------7
I have trouble feeling and   I am a strong empathizer
verbalizing other's pain   and communicator

⇒ How biased are you about what a leader is "supposed to look like?"

1------------2-------------3-------------4-------------5-------------6-------------7
Leader = tall, white, man   Anyone can be a leader

⇒ Great Jazz musicians bring out the best in their band mates...how well do you inspire your team to meet their full potential?

1------------2-------------3-------------4-------------5-------------6-------------7
Others stoop to my level   I always bring out the best in others

2. Reflect

⇒ What change is the "Man in the Mirror" asking you to make to be a better leader?

_____

_____

_____

_____

_____

⇒ If you were to "Imagine" a different future for your organization, what would it look like?

_____

_____

_____

_____

_____

_____

_____

⇒ What makes you "Get Up, Stand Up" as a leader?

_____

_____

_____

_____

_____

_____

_____

3. Commit to New Growth

⇒ Given this article's lessons, what is one simple thing (OST) you will do to practice better leadership?

_____

_____

_____

_____

_____

_____

_____

About the Author

 David Spungin is a Corporate Trainer, Speaker, and Executive Coach focused on transforming managers into high-performing leaders. He holds a degree in Leadership Development from the United States Military Academy at West Point, a Master of Science in Organization Development from American University/The National Training Laboratories for Applied Behavioral Science (NTL), and has completed advanced leadership studies at Harvard University. A U.S. Army combat veteran with corporate leadership experience, he founded The Leader Growth Group in 2014 to develop self-aware leaders who inspire engaged workplaces. He now consults to primarily Fortune 500 companies to include Google, Schlumberger, Accenture, Harris Corporation, Arthur Gallagher, Johns Manville, Hogan Lovells, and Facebook.

As a trainer, David is recognized for his ability to quickly assess an organization's needs, develop creative learning designs, and facilitate highly engaging training events. He's known for his skill in **relating with a wide variety of personalities and cultures**. David can successfully deliver training to an oil and gas services executive team in Alaska one day, and front-line Millennial leaders in Silicon Valley the next. Regardless of the uniqueness of an organization or audience, **David adapts and connects**.

As a coach, David's fit is more specific. His coaching style is what he describes as "**brutal compassion**." He strives to push his clients beyond their comfort zone while simultaneously providing a supporting and trusting environment to take the risks needed to grow. He tends to work best with executives who are analytical, value directness, and who demand practicality from their coaching experience. David specializes in helping leaders to develop their **executive presence**, create **highly trusting and accountable teams**, and building **empathy** and a **servant's approach to leadership** that inspires results.

David is originally from Fairfax, VA and currently resides in Evergreen, CO.

The Leader Growth Group

Email David directly at dspungin@leadergrowthgroup.com

Visit the Leader Growth Group, LLC. website at www.leadergrowthgroup.com

Follow David's blog at http://davidspungin.com/

Connect with David on LinkedIn at https://www.linkedin.com/in/davidspungin

Follow David on Twitter at https://twitter.com/davidspungin

Follow LGG on Facebook at https://www.facebook.com/leadergrowthgroup

Acknowledgements

There have been a few extraordinary teachers in my life that I'd like to acknowledge. These are the professors, trainers, and consultants who generously shared their insights on leadership and pushed me to hone my own ideas. I am forever grateful to: Joseph LeBoeuf, Scott Snook, Julio Olalla, Stuart Heller, Katherine Farquhar, Enrique Zaldivar, Anastasia Bukashe, Ruth Wagner, Alan Klein, Cliff Kayser, Patricia Parham, Peter F. DiGiammarino, Hile Rutledge, Sukari Pinnock, Robert Marshak, Peggy Holman, Ron Heifetz, and Marty Linsky.

Yet, learning does not just happen in the classroom, and much of what I know about leadership stems from key experiences with my many bosses, peers, and colleagues. In that light, I'd like to thank the following for shaping how I think today: COL (Ret) Joseph Moore, COL (Ret) John Peeler, COL (Ret) Michael Spencer, LTC (Ret) Matt Seifert, CSM David Davenport, Mark LeBusque, Adriano Pianesi, Jill Hufnagel, Dolores Bernardo, the members of AU/NTL Cohort 63, my peers at Catalyst Consulting, and the All-American Leadership team.

I've also had some special coaches and mentors in my life. In fact, the principal reason I am doing this work is mostly due to my interactions with the very talented Bill Carrier. Bill, you inspired me to walk this path and I value your continued mentorship greatly. I've also recently been mentored by thought leader, Mark Hodgson, who told me (very directly, many times, until I finally did it) that I needed to pull this book together. Thanks so much for your motivation, Mark!

Lastly, to my wife and family, thanks so much for your continued support. You not only teach me leadership every day, but also, you inspire me to be a better husband, father, son, and son-in-law.

References

Anderson, D.L. (2010). *Organization development: the process of leading organizational change.* Thousands Oaks, CA: SAGE.

Bennis, W. G. (2003). *On becoming a leader.* New York, NY: Basic Books.

Bradberry, T., & Greaves, J. (2009). *Emotional intelligence 2.0.* San Diego, CA: TalentSmart.

Brothers, C. & Kumar, V. (2015) *Language and the pursuit of leadership excellence: How extraordinary leaders build relationships, shape culture and drive breakthrough results.* Naples, FL: New Possibilities Press.

DePree, M. (1989). *Leadership is an art.* New York: Dell Publishing.

Donnithorne, L. R. (1994). *The West Point way of leadership: from learning principled leadership to practicing it.* New York: Currency Doubleday.

D'Souza, S., & Renner, D. (2014). *Not knowing: the art of turning uncertainty into possibility.* London: LID Publishing Ltd.

Franklin, J. P., & Layden, J. (2007). *Building leaders the West Point way: ten principles from the nations most powerful leadership lab.* Nashville: Thomas Nelson.

Goldsmith, M., & Reiter, M. (2015). *Triggers: creating behavior that lasts--becoming the person you want to be.* New York: Crown Business.

Goleman, D. (2015). *Focus: the hidden driver of excellence.* New York: Harper.

Greenleaf, R.K. (2003). *The servant-leader within: a transformative path.* New York: Paulist Press.

Heifetz, R. A. (2003). *Leadership without easy answers.* Cambridge: Belknap Press.

Heifetz, R., Grashow, A., & Linsky, M. (2009). *The practice of adaptive leadership: tools and tactics for changing your organization and the world.* Boston: Harvard Business Press.

Heifetz, R., & Linsky, M. (2002). *Leadership on the line: staying alive through the dangers of leading.* Boston: Harvard Business Review Press.

Holman, P. (2010). *Engaging emergence: turning upheaval into opportunity*. San Francisco, CA: Berrett-Koehler.

Kryder, S. (2011). *The mind to lead: coaching for calm confident power*. Washington, DC: NeuroLeap Press.

Kotter, J.P. (1996). *Leading change*. Boston, MA: Harvard Business Press.

Leonard, G. (1992). *Mastery: the keys to success and long-term fulfillment*. New York: Plume.

Northouse, P. G., (2013). *Leadership: theory and practice* (6th ed,). Thousands Oaks, CA: SAGE.

Senge, P. (1990) *The fifth discipline: The art & practice of the learning organization*. New York, NY: Random House, Inc.

Seuss, Dr. (1958). *Yertle the turtle, and other stories*. New York: Random House.

Seuss, Dr. (1961) *The sneetches, and other stories*. New York: Random House.

Shein, E. (1992). *Organizational culture and leadership: A dynamic view*. San Francisco, CA: Jossey-Bass.

Sinek, S. (2018). *Leaders eat last*. New York, NY: Portfolio Penguin.

Snair, S. (2004). *West Point leadership lessons: duty, honor, and other management principles*. Naperville, IL: Sourcebooks.

Notes

[1] Heifetz, R., Grashow, A., & Linsky, M. (2009). *The Practice of Adaptive Leadership: Tools and Tactics for Changing Your Organization and the World*, Boston: Harvard Business Press.

[2] Profile - Class of 2018. (2014, August 5). Retrieved from http://www.usma.edu/oir/class%20profiles/class%20of%202018.pdf

[3] Heifetz, R., Grashow, A., & Linsky, M. (2009). *The Practice of Adaptive Leadership: Tools and Tactics for Changing Your Organization and the World*, Boston: Harvard Business Press.

[4] Heifetz, R., & Linsky, M. (2002). *Leadership on the Line: Staying Alive through the Dangers of Leading.* Boston: Harvard Business Review Press.

[5] https://www.nytimes.com/2016/02/28/magazine/what-google-learned-from-its-quest-to-build-the-perfect-team.html

[6] Rock, D. (2008). SCARF: a brain-based model for collaborating with and influencing others. *NeuroLeadershipjournal*, (1). doi:https://www.epa.gov/sites/production/files/2015-09/documents/thurs_georgia_9_10_915_covello.pdf

[7] Rosovsky, J. (2015, November 17). The five keys to a successful Google team. Retrieved from https://rework.withgoogle.com/blog/five-keys-to-a-successful-google-team/

[8] Rock, D. (2008). SCARF: a brain-based model for collaborating with and influencing others. *NeuroLeadershipjournal*, (1). doi:https://www.epa.gov/sites/production/files/2015-09/documents/thurs_georgia_9_10_915_covello.pdf

[9] Seuss, Dr. (1958). *Yertle the Turtle, and Other Stories.* New York: Random House.

[10] Seuss, Dr. (1961) *The Sneetches, and Other Stories.* New York: Random House.

[11] Seuss, Dr. (1961) *The Sneetches, and Other Stories.* New York: Random House.

81676657R00080

Made in the USA
Columbia, SC
25 November 2017